ELL

SHADOWING

as a Catalyst for Change

ELL
SHADOWING
as a Catalyst for Change

IVANNIA SOTO

CORWIN
A SAGE Company

CORWIN
A SAGE Company

FOR INFORMATION:

Corwin
A SAGE Company
2455 Teller Road
Thousand Oaks, California 91320
(800) 233-9936
Fax: (800) 417-2466
www.corwin.com

SAGE Ltd.
1 Oliver's Yard
55 City Road
London EC1Y 1SP
United Kingdom

SAGE India Pvt. Ltd.
B 1/I 1 Mohan Cooperative Industrial Area
Mathura Road, New Delhi 110 044
India

SAGE Asia-Pacific Pte. Ltd.
33 Pekin Street #02-01
Far East Square
Singapore 048763

Acquisitions Editor: Dan Alpert
Associate Editor: Megan Bedell
Editorial Assistant: Sarah Bartlett
Project Editor: Veronica Stapleton
Copy Editors: Julie Meiklejohn & Diane DiMura
Typesetter: C&M Digitals (P) Ltd.
Proofreader: Scott Oney
Indexer: Wendy Allex
Cover Designer: Michael Dubowe
Permissions Editor: Karen Ehrmann

Printed in the United States of America.

Library of Congress Cataloging-in-Publication Data

ELL shadowing as a catalyst for change / Ivannia Soto.

p. cm.
Includes bibliographical references and index.

ISBN 978-1-4129-9206-0 (pbk.)

1. Linguistic minorities—Education—United States.
2. Children with social disabilities—Education—United States. 3. Language arts—Remedial teaching—United States.
4. Individualized instruction—United States.
5. Observation (Educational method) I. Title.

LC3731.S666 2012 371.829073—dc23 2011041177

This book is printed on acid-free paper.

MIX
Paper from
responsible sources
FSC® C012947
www.fsc.org

18 19 20 2 1 10 9 8 7 6 5 4

Contents

Additional materials and resources related to *ELL Shadowing as a Catalyst for Change* can be found at http://www.corwin.com/ellshadowing

Acknowledgments

Words cannot express the depth of gratitude that I have for everyone who played a part in the development of this book. Special thanks to my family and friends who have been with me throughout the journey of writing this book. I am especially grateful to my mother, Blanca Estela Soto, who always told me that I could do anything that I set my mind to do; my sister, Arlene Soto Smith, whom I call my first and best writing teacher; and my father, Rodrigo Soto, for modeling how to plan ahead in life (and now in writing).

I am also indebted to Dr. Linda J. Carstens, who was integral in developing the English Language Learner (ELL) Shadowing process and has been my mentor and friend for as long as ELL shadowing has now existed. This was the book that I wanted to write with you, Linda, and you left a huge legacy of ELL shadowing in my hands. I hope that I have done it justice.

This book came out of an innovative and magical time for professional learning and development in District 6 of the Los Angeles Unified School District. A variety of district office members, including Dr. Dale Vigil, Glynn Thompson, Edward Manson, Cindy Paulos, and David Manzo, helped lead the effort. I am grateful to have been able to work with and learn so much from each of you during that time in my life.

I am also grateful to my home institution, Whittier College, for supporting the development of this book and the accompanying instructional video clips via generous faculty development grants. Thanks are specifically in order to my research assistant and former student, Kathy Villalón, for her assistance with inputting edits to the first draft and working on figures, as well as to Aiddee Tellez, Student Teaching Services/Graduate Admissions clerk, who assisted with source references and permissions.

Special thanks to both Norwalk–La Mirada Unified School District in Norwalk, California, and Lucia Mar Unified School in Arroyo Grande, California, for being supportive of ELL shadowing in your districts. In Norwalk–La Mirada Unified School District, many thanks go to Superintendent Dr. Ruth Peréz for approving ELL shadowing at a variety of school sites, as well as Rosa Carreón, Categorical Program Director, and Mi Lee, ELL Teacher on Special Assignment, for being committed to ELL work, including ELL shadowing, within the district every day. Special thanks to Principal Dr. Gloria Jimenez and Vice-Principal Michelle Owen at Los Alisos Middle School, as well as to teacher-leaders Mr. Jose Manso, Ms. Stephanie Rizo, and Mr. Marvin Soto for also being a part of the videotaping project. And a thank you to Principal Rudy Gonzaléz at Morrison Elementary School, as well as Ms. Sheryl Edwards, Ms. Irene Mesa, and Ms. Jennifer Murrey, for providing demonstration lessons, which are also part of the video project. Lastly, thank you to Dr. Ligia Hallstrom, Principal of John Glenn High School, as well as teachers Mr. Patrick Flynn and Mr. Michael Stave, who provided videotape footage at the high school level.

Many thanks to Lucia Mar Unified School District, including Assistant Superintendent Andy Stenson, Categorical Director Barbara La Coco, and especially ELL Teacher on Special Assignment Ann Markarian for being so invested in ELL shadowing in your district. Thank you, Ann, for organizing each ELL shadowing training by putting together the student profiles and resource materials as well as attending each district and school site ELL shadowing training that has been conducted. In a few short years, you have set a firm foundation and leveraged resources and talent within Lucia Mar to create instructional access for ELLs. I am also grateful to the central coast of California for providing writing inspiration throughout the year and a half that it took to write this book.

Finally, thank you to all of the county offices of education in California where ELL shadowing has been featured, including Stanislaus County, Kern County, Santa Barbara County, and San Luis Obispo County Offices of Education. Special thanks must also be given to Teresa Iniguez-Vega, former ELL coordinator at the San Luis Obispo County Office of Education, for revising the ELL shadowing protocol so that it is more user-friendly for all participants.

PUBLISHER'S ACKNOWLEDGMENTS

Corwin gratefully acknowledges the contributions of the following reviewers:

Nana Almers, Instructional Manager
Department of Language and Cultural Equity
Albuquerque Public Schools
Albuquerque, NM

Linda J. Carstens, Director of Professional Development
Stanford University
Stanford, CA

Bobbianne Ericson, Facilitator, Staff Development
El Paso Independent School District
El Paso, TX

Diane Staehr Fenner, Education Consultant, ELL
DSF Consulting, LLC
Fairfax, VA

Margery Ginsberg, Associate Professor
Leadership for Learning Program
College of Education
University of Washington, Seattle
Seattle, WA

Casey L. Gordon, ELL/Languages/Homeless Coordinator
Kent Intermediate School District
Grand Rapids, MI

Marsha Guerrero, Principal
Morrison Elementary School
Norwalk, CA

Olga M. Hickman, Senior Field Trainer
Texas Institute for the Acquisition of Language for Learning
Meadows Center for Preventing Educational Risk
University of Texas at Austin
Austin, TX

Bobbi Ciriza Houtchens, Teacher/ELL Staff Development
National Education Association/Los Angeles County Office of Education
Teaching Ambassador Fellow, U.S. Department of Education
Los Angeles/Washington, D.C.

Teresa Vega-Iniquez, ELL Coordinator
San Luis Obispo County Office of Education
San Luis Obispo, CA

Jen Paul, ELL Consultant
Bureau of Educational Assessment & Accountability
Michigan Department of Education
Ann Arbor, MI

Tiffany S. Powell, Office of Diversity Coordinator
Manhattan-Ogden USD 383
Manhattan, KS

Sandra Rodriguez
Department of Language and Cultural Equity
Albuquerque Public Schools
Albuquerque, NM

Arlene Soto Smith, English Teacher
Sierra High School
Whittier, CA

Dr. Katherine Sprott, Program Coordinator
Midwest Equity Assistance Center Office of the Dean
Kansas State University
Manhattan, KS

Lynn Shafer Willner, ELL Specialist and Senior Research Scientist
The George Washington University
Center for Equity and Excellence in Education
Arlington, VA

About the Author

 **Dr. Ivannia Soto** is Associate Professor of Education at Whittier College, where she specializes in second language acquisition, systemic reform for English Language Learners (ELLs), and urban education. She began her career in the Los Angeles Unified School District (LAUSD), where she taught English and English language development to a population made up of 99.9 percent Latinos who either were or had been ELLs. Before becoming a professor, Dr. Soto also served the Los Angeles Unified School District as a literacy coach and district office administrator. She has presented on literacy and language topics at various conferences, including the National Association for Bilingual Education (NABE), the California Association for Bilingual Association (CABE), the New York State Association for Bilingual Education (NYSABE), and the National Urban Education Conference. As a consultant, Soto has worked with Stanford University's School Redesign Network (SRN) and WestEd, as well as a variety of districts and county offices in California, providing technical assistance for systemic reform for ELLs and Title III. She is the coauthor of *The Literacy Gaps: Building Bridges for ELLs and SELs*, her first book with Corwin, and the author of a variety of articles on providing appropriate instructional access for ELLs.

Introduction

My parents, Blanca Estela Artavia Soto and Rodrigo Soto, immigrated to the United States from Costa Rica—my mother when she was eleven years old and my father when he was twenty-one years old. Their story, like that of many children of immigrants, is central to my work with schools and in teacher education, as well as to my research passions now as an adult. My mother went to school in the Los Angeles Unified School District during a time when a systemic plan for working with English Language Learners (ELLs) was uncharted territory. Although she spent many more years in United States schools than in Costa Rican schools, in high school she quickly noticed that she was not developing the English language skills that she would need to become proficient. Being the self-starter that she was (and still is), my mother became her own advocate and enrolled herself in additional adult school English classes in order to receive the English language instruction that she needed and deserved. It is because of her persistence and determination that my sister, Arlene Soto Smith, and I have furthered ourselves in this country as we have.

Unfortunately, this notion of not systemically meeting the instructional needs of our ELLs still exists today. Although we now have a strong body of research literature pointing toward best practices with ELLs, and even though we have more and more district, state, and federal policies in place to meet the instructional needs of ELLs, the same inequities that my mother contended with over fifty-one years ago continue to prevail. Such imbalances fuel my work. When I review data and see that the achievement gap still exists, read articles about the politics of why we are not educationally advancing the way we need to, or work with districts that are in state sanction because they are not making adequate yearly progress with their ELLs, I refuse to stop trying to create change within systems. Part of the reason is when I see all of these issues in education, I see them through the lens of one person—my mother—and that keeps me going. That is the purpose of ELL shadowing—reflecting upon a day in the life of a child or adolescent in English language transition who may be experiencing school slightly differently than native English speakers.

Throughout this book you will get to know one ELL named Josue. Although he is a compilation of all of the ELLs that I have shadowed, he represents the invisibility and silence that many of our ELLs experience in school. But Josue, like my mother before him, has a story; he must be allowed to gain voice and an academic identity in the classroom setting. He needs to be engaged and heard and understood in the classroom. He has so much to say if we would only elicit his speech and listen . . . Remember Josue each time you use this book. You will never teach the same way again—I promise.

SECTION I

Purpose of Shadowing

1

Creating a Sense of Urgency

According to recent findings by the Reparable Harm Report (Olsen, 2010), the majority of secondary school English Language Learners are "Long-Term English Learners (LTELs)," defined as English Language Learners (ELLs) who have been in the United States for more than six years but haven't reached sufficient English proficiency or attained adequate academic gains in grade-level content. Due to their LTEL status, many ELL students are relegated to watered-down curriculum that will not prepare them for college and beyond. Instead of being given the intensive academic language support to meet the rigorous demands of grade-level content, far too many ELLs are thought to be cognitively unable to do more than their language fluency allows them to demonstrate. Also, ELLs have historically been allowed to be silent and invisible, as their cultural norms often keep them quiet and compliant in classroom settings. Currently, this is a pandemic issue in California, where one in three districts has a student population with 75 percent of their ELLs considered to be LTELs. But this must also sound the alarm and create awareness for districts and schools across the country before it is too late (Olsen, 2010). The issues of an inequitable education for some is also part of what U.S. Secretary of Education Arne Duncan (2010) has termed the "new civil rights": the achievement gap between groups of children—Latinos, African Americans, and ELLs compared with native English learners—is a moral and ethical imperative. As educators, we should not only want to close the achievement gap in order to get out of federal sanctions. We should want to do this because it is the future that every child needs and deserves. As W. E. B. Du Bois suggested in 1949 in *The Freedom to Learn* and Linda Darling-Hammond reminded us in 1997 in her similarly titled book, *The Right to Learn*,

> of all the civil rights for which the world has struggled and fought for 5,000 years, the right to learn is undoubtedly the most fundamental. . . . The freedom to learn . . . has been bought by bitter sacrifice. And whatever we may think of the curtailment of other civil rights, we should fight to the last ditch to keep open the right to learn, the right to have examined in our schools not only what we believe, but what we do not believe; not only what our leaders say, but what the leaders of other groups and nations, and the leaders of other centuries have said. We must insist upon this to give our children the fairness of a start which will equip them with such an array of facts and such an attitude toward truth that they can have a real chance to judge what the world is and what its greater minds have thought it might be. (p. 1)

We cannot and must not rest until every group of students receives the kind of education that they deserve. This book will remind the reader of a group currently struggling with inequity within the U.S. educational system, ELLs. It will also propose a way to create systemic urgency for this group of students, using both processes for change and an instructional strategy called ELL shadowing. ELL shadowing is a professional development design that involves a single teacher observing a single ELL during the course of a school day. I often describe the process as experiencing a day in the life of an ELL by taking a snapshot of his or her speaking and active listening experiences every five minutes over the course of two hours. This process becomes a powerful way to shed light on the specific linguistic and cultural needs of ELLs. ELL shadowing, in conjunction with follow-up professional development, allows educators to begin to create systemic instructional access and equity for ELLs.

PREPARING TEACHERS TO INSTRUCT ELLS

Teachers go into teaching with good intentions. But somehow the demands of the classroom—sometimes the size, the lack of resources, or the variability in language ability level—begin to wear on educators. These demands are coupled with the fact that teacher education and preservice programs are not doing enough to train teachers to meet the linguistic and cultural needs of this very specific student population (Wei, Darling-Hammond, Andree, Richardson, & Orphanos, 2009). California, for example, with its surge in ELL numbers, has moved toward an embedded certification process, requiring, in most colleges and universities, one course that addresses the needs of ELLs while also integrating topics focusing on ELLs into the rest of the teacher preparation coursework. In other words, teachers in California come out of teacher preparation programs with an ELL certification as part of their overall credentialing process. While this looks like a positive concept at the outset because all teachers become certified to teach ELLs, teachers no longer have to take additional coursework outside of their credentials to teach ELLs. Although every teacher is required to complete minimal coursework to teach ELLs, this is hardly enough to become effective with the specific needs of ELLs or the demands that teachers experience in the field once they are required to teach them. Although California is unique in this approach to preparing mainstream teachers to teach ELLs, the fact that the majority of states do not require such certification also demonstrates a need for focused and ongoing professional development on the specific needs of this group of students. Both preservice and inservice training about the needs of ELLs is needed to create systemic instructional and achievement change.

Focused and Ongoing Professional Development on ELLs

In addition to preservice training, teachers also need focused, sustained, and aligned professional development once they enter the field. If preservice teachers are receiving only one course focused on the needs of ELLs, and others receive no such course at all, then all teachers need additional opportunities to refine their scaffolding skills with ELLs once they enter the teaching field. According to findings from Learning Forward (formerly known as the National Staff Development Council), "Teachers are not getting adequate training in teaching special education or limited English proficiency students. More than two-thirds of teachers nationally had not had even one day of training in supporting the learning of special education or LEP [ELL] students during the previous three years" (Wei et al., 2009, p. 6). Specifically, teachers would benefit from both a series of courses and a variety of course work experiences that sensitize them to meet the specific linguistic and cultural needs of ELLs in our schools. Additionally, when teachers enter their classrooms, ongoing and focused professional development that supports them in best meeting the needs of ELLs and scaffolding instruction for this group of students is paramount to closing students' literacy gaps (Soto-Hinman & Hetzel, 2009). Learning Forward also suggests that teachers need close to fifty hours of professional development to improve their skills and their students' learning. This means that teacher learning must also be ongoing. Professional development must be focused, aligned, and coherent. It should not change from year to year or when the new flavor of the month appears. Teachers need time to become skilled at practices that will improve student achievement. Professional development should also be data driven, connected to the specific needs of students at a school site, and, therefore, personalized.

As Darling-Hammond (2009) suggests,

> Teacher qualifications, teacher's knowledge and skills, make more difference for student learning than any other single factor. Clearly,

this means that if we want to improve student learning, what we have to do is invest in teachers' learning. We have to be sure that teachers understand not only their content area, which is very important, but also, how do students learn? How do different students learn differently? How do students acquire language? How do second language learners need to be taught?

In this way, both preservice and inservice training must become more focused and aligned in both the course work and field work opportunities required, in order to ensure appropriate cultural and linguistic differentiation for ELLs. The ELL shadowing project is one way to provide a focused and sustained effort around the academic oral language development and listening needs of ELLs within a system.

What Is the ELL Shadowing Project?

The ELL shadowing project is a way to create urgency around the instructional and linguistic needs of ELLs, either in teacher training or in staff development. The process allows teachers to see firsthand, in classrooms that look like their own, the sense of urgency that exists when the specific needs of ELLs are not addressed systemically. There are different kinds of ELLs—newcomers who are highly literate, educated, or underschooled; long-term ELLs who have been in the country six years or longer; and ELLs progressing predictably through the developmental sequence. It is imperative to tailor professional development and instruction to the specific needs of the ELLs at a school site (Olsen, 2006). With the ELL shadowing project, this means that if most ELLs at a particular school or district lay at the midrange of English language proficiency, students at that level of language progression should be tracked for the ELL shadowing experience. This will allow the system to draw attention to that particular level of proficiency need while encouraging everyone to focus on that one specific group for a particular period of time. Educators will then also be able to target follow-up professional development sessions and focus on instructional strategies for that specific group of ELLs. The time of random acts of strategy usage should be gone, and we must instead tailor instruction to data collected on gaps in instruction. The ELL shadowing project is a way to triangulate achievement data with classroom observations to better serve the academic needs of ELLs.

The ELL shadowing project also allows all teachers within a system— whether it be grade level or department, entire school, district, or county office—to focus on the specific needs of an ELL through the lens of one child. Systems often do not get the opportunity to reflect on their practices and focus their efforts in one direction. The ELL shadowing project is an opportunity to do so over a two-day period to begin a new systemic vision for change with this group of students.

The ELL shadowing project allows professional development to be focused and directed to the specific needs of the ELL population being served within a system. Since specific classroom data on academic speaking and listening is collected through the ELL shadowing project, subsequent professional development can be differentiated and tailored so that the academic needs of ELLs within that particular system are met. In most districts and schools across the country, the needs of ELL populations are expansive, so the professional development and focus on this population of students must also be ongoing to properly address those needs. After the ELL shadowing project, there must be follow-up training on how to address the linguistic and cultural needs of this population of students so that ELLs begin to make the kind of progress needed to become proficient in English and academic content.

ELL Shadowing for Progress Monitoring

ELL shadowing can also be used regularly for progress monitoring when awareness has been created around a certain group at a particular level. For example, once follow-up professional development has been provided for teachers on how to create more academic oral language development in the classroom setting, teachers can visit each other's classrooms in order to monitor and learn from student engagement strategies being used. If professional development has been offered around incorporating productive group work structures, teachers can visit each other's classrooms to learn from colleagues to determine if the amount of listening and speaking has increased by using specific academic oral language development instructional strategies. In this way, ELL shadowing can be used alongside existing professional development structures, including instructional coaching models, Professional Learning Communities (PLCs), Response to Intervention (RTI), or Sheltered Instruction Observation Protocol (SIOP). The ELL shadowing project can enhance and accompany other initiatives by placing a spotlight on the needs of ELLs within a system. Once specific needs have been determined for ELLs using the shadowing experience, existing structures that are in place can be used alongside the initiative to assist with sustaining instructional change. If existing structures are currently not in place, there are suggestions for creating such structures in Chapter 10 of this book.

What ELL Shadowing Is Not

It is important to note that ELL shadowing is not intended to be the be-all and end-all—it is not a panacea or a silver bullet. ELL shadowing is the beginning of awareness and focus on the specific academic literacy needs of ELLs, but educators often don't view their classrooms and students in the same way after having had the experience. After a recent ELL shadowing training in Lucia Mar Unified School District in Arroyo Grande, California, where ninety teachers and administrators were in attendance, educators reflected in their evaluation of the training with comments like "I will never look at classroom instruction the same again," "This is the most powerful professional development I have ever been through," and "I think that shadowing should be done every year to reflect on our teaching" (confidential training evaluations, 2010).

Still, the ELL shadowing project is only the first step in creating systemic achievement and instructional change for ELLs within a system. Once the ELL shadowing project itself has been completed, ongoing and sustained follow-up professional development must also be provided so that teachers then know *how* to change instructional practices in their classrooms for ELLs. As suggested earlier, fifty hours of sustained and consistent professional development over time is needed in order to begin to change teacher practice (Wei et al., 2009). This book contributes to teacher development by providing (1) ways of shadowing an ELL in order to create urgency and (2) specific instructional strategies to change systemic practices and scaffold instruction via academic language development techniques once ELL shadowing has been completed.

ORGANIZATION OF THE BOOK

Throughout the book, we follow one ELL student named Josue. Although a pseudonym has been used, Josue is a compilation of many ELLs that I have shadowed since 2003. Chapter 2 introduces the history and context of ELL shadowing, with its inception in the Los Angeles Unified School District's (LAUSD) Local District 6. Chapter 3 provides a mini case study about Josue with specific emphasis on the classroom observation of this ELL. Josue's achievement results have been included both in Chapter 3 and in Chapter 6. We also follow Josue's progress in listening and academic speaking throughout several chapters (academic speaking in Chapters 4 and 7 and academic listening in Chapters 5 and 7). You will find some redundancy in the book. That is intentional in order to ensure a clear understanding of how to complete the ELL shadowing project. In this way, Chapter 4 provides the research base for academic oral language development but also introduces how to use the ELL shadowing protocol for academic language specifically. Similarly, in Chapter 5, the reader is introduced to the importance of teaching academic listening explicitly as well as how to use the protocol for listening specifically. Chapter 6 presents an overview of the logistics of setting up an ELL shadowing training in a school, district, or county. In Chapter 7, the reader will find a detailed overview of how to use all portions of the ELL shadowing protocol to ensure that the process is adhered to with fidelity. Chapter 8 discusses how to analyze results from an ELL shadowing project, and Chapter 9 introduces how a system might leverage change based on the ELL shadowing experience. Finally, Chapter 10 discusses what to do after the ELL shadowing experience, including strategy suggestions for ways to elicit more academic oral language development and listening in a classroom setting. The accompanying online video clips present classroom teachers in diverse classrooms implementing Think-Pair-Share for listening and speaking, productive group work for listening and speaking, and the Frayer Model for vocabulary development.

This book is also primarily based on the text *Scaffolding Language, Scaffolding Learning* by Pauline Gibbons (2002), in which she discusses how to scaffold the literacy domains of speaking, listening, reading, and writing with ELLs. The ELL shadowing experience is primarily based on the speaking (Chapter 2) and listening (Chapter 6) chapters of Gibbons's text, as these are the two domains that educators will monitor when they engage in shadowing. Although other literature has been cited, the ELL shadowing project was created as a culminating experience after a book study on the Gibbons text in 2003 in District 6 of the LAUSD. More about the historical context of ELL shadowing can be read in Chapter 3.

This book is not intended to be the only source for reading on the importance of academic literacy with ELLs. Additional study groups during PLCs or department or grade-level meetings can be formed after the ELL shadowing project in order to extend knowledge of academic oral language development and active listening. Similarly, the academic oral language development definition and instructional strategies outlined in Chapter 10 are starting points for systemic change, but they are not intended to be the only definition or strategies used.

As you read about Josue throughout this book, think about an ELL in your own classroom. When you shadow an ELL, think about what you might do differently in your own classroom the very next day. Thinking about what you do every day to scaffold instruction for ELLs will assist not only in closing the achievement gap but also in creating instructional access for ELLs in their academic futures.

REFERENCES

Darling-Hammond, L. (1997). *The right to learn: A blueprint for creating schools that work.* San Francisco, CA: Jossey-Bass.

Darling-Hammond, L. (2009). *Linda Darling-Hammond: Thoughts on teacher preparation.* Retrieved from http://www.edutopia.org/ldh-teacher-preparation

Du Bois, W.E.B. (1949). "The Freedom to Learn." In P. S. Foner (Ed.), *W.E.B. Du Bois Speaks*, 230–231.

Duncan, A. (2010, July). *Equity and education reform.* Remarks at the annual meeting of the National Association for the Advancement of Colored People (NAACP).

Gibbons, P. (2002). *Scaffolding language, scaffolding learning: Teacher second language learners in the mainstream classroom.* Portsmouth, NH: Heinemann.

Olsen, L. (2006). Ensuring academic success for English learners. *University of California Linguistic Minority Research Institute Newsletter, 15*(4), 1–7.

Olsen, L. (2010). *Reparable harm: Fulfilling the unkept promise of educational opportunity for California's long-term English learners.* Long Beach, CA: Californians Together.

Soto-Hinman, I., & Hetzel, J. (2009). *The literacy gaps: Building bridges for English language learners and standard English learners.* Thousand Oaks, CA: Corwin.

Wei, R. C., Darling-Hammond, L., Andree, A., Richardson, N., & Orphanos, S. (2009). *Professional learning in the learning profession: A status report on teacher development in the United States and abroad.* Dallas, TX: National Staff Development Council.

2

History and Context of Shadowing

The power of English Language Learner (ELL) shadowing is in the student. As educators within educational systems, we do not often have the opportunity to observe one child and experience instruction from that child's perspective. In this manner, the power of ELL shadowing is in the opportunity to come together as a system to observe the needs of ELLs through the same lens and then have the opportunity to discuss what was viewed from the standpoint of one ELL. ELL shadowing is a catalyst by which all educators within a system can align and become clearer around the specific needs of ELLs within their particular context or setting, whether it is at a school site, within a district, or at the county level. Usually we go into classrooms to observe or evaluate teachers. The purpose of ELL shadowing is to observe a day in the instructional life of one ELL. When you go into a classroom full to the brim with thirty students, it is easy to place blame or be overwhelmed by the sheer numbers. When you look at the instructional needs of one child or one adolescent at a time, it is difficult to turn away. As educators, we become connected again, and the reasons that we went into education are realized anew.

The first ELL shadowing project was conducted in 2003 in Local District 6 of the Los Angeles Unified School District (LAUSD) and stemmed from the work of an ELL task force made up of district administrators and content specialists. I was a literacy specialist working closely with a consultant to Local District 6 named Dr. Linda J. Carstens. Together, we, as well as a small group of interested members, designed professional development experiences in order to bring coherence and alignment to the needs of ELLs within their district. The ELL shadowing protocol itself was built around the 2002 work of Pauline Gibbons's *Scaffolding Language, Scaffolding Learning*. After Local District 6 administrators had completed a book study around the Gibbons text, they decided that they wanted a culminating exercise that would allow them to apply their new learning about ELLs in context. The ELL shadowing protocol was designed specifically from Chapters 2 and 6 of the Gibbons text, which discuss the academic oral language, or speaking needs, of ELLs as well as the listening demands of this student group. Both academic speaking and listening are underdeveloped domains that scaffold what are considered the literacy domains of reading and writing. If educators develop the academic speaking of ELLs, they are assisting with the development of student writing, as both speaking and writing are about output or production. As August and Shanahan (2006) suggest, speaking is the foundation of literacy for ELLs. Similarly, both listening and reading are about input or receptive skills. When we require ELLs to actively listen, we are modeling and scaffolding active reading processes. It is important to reinforce and provide professional development around these two literacy domains before an educator ever enters a classroom to shadow an ELL (this is reinforced in Chapters 4 and 5 of this book) so that a participant understands what he or she is observing during the ELL shadowing experience. This process, in these stages, allows educators to have the same lens and alignment around what is being observed in a classroom setting.

ELL shadowing, then, is a technique for examining specific areas of an ELL's schooling experience and gaining insight into the student's perspective about school. The shadowing project involves selecting an ELL (the selection can be at random or at a predetermined English language proficiency level) and following the student for two to three hours, noting academic speaking and listening experiences at every five-minute interval. The purpose of student shadowing is to gather information about the daily life of an ELL, in order to participate in a larger conversation on improving the educational experiences of this group of students. The experience begins at the individual ELL student level because as educators within educational systems, we look at groups of students and subgroups, but we often do not have the opportunity to observe the instructional experiences of individual students. Many times, we become overwhelmed by the specific linguistic and cultural needs of subgroups of students, and it is easier to turn away. The group results from the ELL shadowing experience can certainly be generalized and leveraged, as patterns and themes are analyzed, but it is first essential to explore what it is like to go through school needing to do "double the work"—that is, processing both language and content.

In a school or district context, teachers may engage in ELL shadowing projects in which they follow a student at a particular English language proficiency level for several hours. Educators are invited to gain an understanding regarding the student's academic oral language and listening needs as experienced through the process, while obtaining qualitative data about the student's academic life through the specific comments documented. Such ELL shadowing projects have been conducted in several universities in Southern California, including Whittier College, Biola University, and Claremont Graduate University; in a variety of California school districts, including the Los Angeles Unified School District, Norwalk–La Mirada Unified School District, Lucia Mar Unified School District, Hayward Unified School District; in the Albuquerque, New Mexico, Public Schools; and in several California county education offices, including Stanislaus, Kern, Santa Barbara, and San Luis Obispo County Offices of Education. All of these training sessions were provided in order to have preservice teachers and inservice educators gain a glimpse into a day in the life of hundreds of ELLs in these local school settings. The power of ELL shadowing at the county office level can be viewed using the Stanislaus, California, County Office of Education online video clip.

ELL SHADOWING PROCESSES

During Day 1 of the professional development session, participants are trained using a protocol in which they are taught how to monitor the domains of listening and academic speaking at five-minute intervals for at least two consecutive hours. It is important to note that participants are not ready to formally shadow ELLs until they have studied both the elements of academic talk and the different forms of listening in the classroom, which they will later monitor in a classroom setting (see Chapters 4 and 5). In a professional development setting, participants do not shadow an ELL until the morning of Day 2 after they have amply studied academic speaking and listening on Day 1 of the training. Figure 2.1 is a sample ELL shadowing schedule.

This process of preparation for ELL shadowing on Day 1 of professional development ensures reliability of data collection while making sure that everyone is on the same page regarding what they are observing in the classroom setting. In the end, the research that is presented and strategies that are modeled when participants are trained to shadow become the very techniques needed in the classroom in order to work toward systemically changing the absence of academic oral language development and structured listening in classrooms. Chapter 3 describes my first ELL shadowing experience, including the analysis of student achievement data, the classroom observation, and the debriefing of the experience.

Figure 2.1 Sample English Language Learner (ELL) Shadowing Schedule

ELL Shadowing Schedule	
Day One: Preparation for Shadowing	**Day Two: Shadowing at Schools and Debrief**
• AM—Speaking and Listening Session	• AM—ELL Shadowing at School Sites ○ Preparation/review of materials at school site
• PM—How to Use the ELL Shadowing Protocol ○ Detail regarding school assignments and ELL students	• PM—Debriefing the ELL Shadowing Experience and Next Steps for Systems

REFERENCES

August, D., & Shanahan, T. (2006). *Developing literacy in second-language learners: Report of the national literacy panel on language minority children and youth.* Mahwah, NJ: Lawrence Erlbaum Associates.

Gibbons, P. (2002). *Scaffolding language, scaffolding learning: Teaching second language learners in the mainstream classroom.* Portsmouth, NH: Heinemann.

3

A Day in the Life of Josue, an English Language Learner

According to Fix, Mc Hugh, Terrazas, and Laglagaron (2008), a 2006 report by the National Migration Institute indicated that a large percentage of English Language Learners (ELLs)—64 percent—were born in the United States. Josue, the first student I ever shadowed, was no different. He was in the tenth grade, and by the time our paths crossed at one of the largest high schools in California with a total population of 5,600 students, he had been in U.S. schools for eleven years. I met Josue first on paper, as I had been given his most recent school picture so that I could identify him when I got into his first period classroom. In the picture provided, Josue wore a sweatshirt with a hood and a white T-shirt underneath—what seemed to be typical teenage attire. He had the beginnings of a mustache, which traced over a bit of a smile along his lips. His eyes seemed kind as they peered out at me from the photo, something that I would confirm when I first saw Josue in person in the classroom setting. His eyes, however, seemed to want to say more than he could or was able to say. This was perhaps the voicelessness and invisibility that he had learned to get by with in the classroom setting. In his school picture, Josue appeared to somehow be making himself smaller as he hunched over a bit—it was as if he was there but not really fully there.

STUDENT PROFILE OF JOSUE

When I found Josue in his classroom, his eyes gazed beyond the walls of his classroom and teacher, to activities (perhaps soccer?). For most of the class session, Josue was slumped over, staring at his textbook, perhaps hoping that the answers and learning would become clearer for him if he only looked longer or harder. As I analyzed his grades from the profile form provided by the school, I noticed that Josue struggled most with the subject areas that I would shadow him in—Algebra and Biology. At the time, Josue was in a four-semester Algebra I course in which he had received a *C* and a two-year biology course in which he had earned a *D*. Both courses were labeled as "sheltered," meaning that content should be taught alongside language. In the classrooms in which I shadowed Josue, there was little content or language going on as the students were virtually teaching themselves. Instead of receiving the intensive instruction and direct support that he needed, Josue sat through mindless exercises and silent worksheets. Both seemed to suck the life out of the joy of learning for him, but still he persevered. According to his attendance records, he had only missed one day of school that year and his teachers stated that he "behaved well."

Achievement Results

Josue's cumulative grade point average (GPA) was 2.9091 (out of 4.0), which was almost a *B* average, even though he had only earned 27.5 credits toward graduation by the tenth grade (most schools in California require between 220 and 230 credits). If Josue wanted to graduate on time, he had some serious catching up to do. Some of the courses that he was taking weren't even *a-g* courses, a sequence of high school courses that students in California must complete with a *C* or better to be *minimally* eligible for admission to the University of California (UC) or the California State University (CSU) system. These courses represent the basic level of academic preparation that high school students should achieve to undertake university work, and still Josue would not be able to meet those minimum expectations. It seemed that before I even entered the classroom, the odds were stacked against Josue.

On the California English Language Development Test (CELDT), which is an English language proficiency assessment, Josue had regressed in achievement over the past three years. His highest scores (on a 1–5 scale) were a 5 in Reading and 4s in Listening and Speaking in 2007, but those scores had slumped down to 3s in Reading and Speaking by 2009. Unfortunately, many ELLs have not been informed of the importance of the CELDT. Many ELLs have seen this assessment once a year since they first entered school but do not take it seriously, especially because many educators also do not realize its importance. In fact, the CELDT is the first hurdle that ELLs must cross before they truly begin to encounter rigorous, grade-level curricula. A study by the Tomas Rivera Policy Institute (2009) suggests that ELLs in the Los Angeles Unified School District (LAUSD) who demonstrated proficiency in English on the CELDT by as late as the eighth grade had significantly improved academic outcomes.

Josue's poor academic scores seemed to be a foreshadowing of what I would see when I observed him in the classroom. Josue did not say one word, not even when he had the opportunity to do so. He also did not receive any direct instruction on the content introduced. Instead, he silently read his textbook and tried to make sense of the material before him. He was, in essence, teaching himself that day, and I wondered how many days like this Josue had had throughout his schooling experience. Perhaps that was why he was not progressing academically as he should have. I had a feeling that the lack of instruction and care around his instructional progress was more the norm as I reviewed the rest of his assessment progress and spent the day in two of his classrooms.

Mini Data Talk

Josue's grade-level assessment result on the California Standards Test (CST) was 331 (out of 450) for English language arts and 279 (out of 450) for mathematics. Both of these scores were in the "Far Below Basic" range, which is not meeting minimum requirements for state or federal accountability progress. Josue had also not yet passed the California High School Exit Exam (CAHSEE), which measures the minimum skills and requirements for graduation in California and which is set at the ninth-grade level. Additionally, out of a class of 519, Josue, even with what seemed to be the least bit of instruction, was right near the middle of his class standing at 271. With these kinds of scores, it seemed that the instructional damage that had been done to Josue was also going on for others.

Period 1: Algebra I

I first "met" Josue in his first period algebra class on a gloomy day in May. The class was working on a math worksheet that was based on the textbook, a newly adopted text in this particular district. Josue carefully and quietly moved his eyes from the textbook to the worksheet for the entire hour that he was in this class. Even as others around him worked with partners or in groups in which students taught each other, Josue chose to work alone. I wasn't close enough to tell if he was completing his worksheet correctly, but Josue seemed to be exerting a lot of effort and mental energy on the document. Several times, other students came over to Josue to ask him a question and engage him, but even after he exchanged a few words with them, he always seemed to prefer to work on his own, as the group work was not structured or required. It was as if Josue had been trained to be silent and compliant. The rest of the class went like this for Josue: he quietly fixated on that worksheet as if he thought that if he looked at it just one more time, he would suddenly understand it. By the end of the period, no direct instruction had taken place. Instead, the teacher merely walked around the room, providing assistance to the students who asked for help. The entire class of students, really, seemed to be teaching themselves. But ELLs like Josue seemed to struggle the most as they were already far behind and had no time to waste on individual activities that were not deliberately crafted to allow them access to content and language at the same time. Josue did not need to complete twenty math problems quietly, a task that required only rote memory in silence. Instead, he needed to be challenged to think critically and problem-solve around culturally relevant math problems (Soto-Hinman & Hetzel, 2009). Josue needed contextualized instruction instead of lecture and silence, as well as the opportunity to work out math problems in a hands-on manner. Most of all, Josue needed to practice his academic language in mathematics to prepare him for the linguistic and content demands of life in college and the workplace.

Period 2: Biology

Josue's second period biology class was not much better. Here, he watched a video on skin cancer and the epidermis. The visual depictions in the video clearly connected to the content that had been taught, but the vocabulary and lack of structured listening over an entire period proved to be difficult for Josue as well as the rest of the class. Josue watched the video respectfully, perhaps making sense of some of the content. I watched Josue nod off a bit during the video, while several other students began to discuss unrelated topics toward the end of the period, but the teacher seemed satisfied that his teaching had been done for the day. With a little assistance, this lesson could have been helpful to Josue and his classmates. I could not help thinking that perhaps a listening guide could have been included with specific content or key vocabulary that Josue needed to actively listen for. The teacher could have started the class with a warm-up or "sponge" activity, encouraging students to discuss key points from the chapter they had just gone over. Students could have also stopped and pair-shared around key concepts during specific times in the video. Finally, Josue could have been required to reflect on his learning by completing an exit slip at the end of class, on which he would have written down key ideas he had learned from the video and questions he still had. All of these techniques would provide scaffolds for Josue and the rest of the class and accountability for the learning that took place via the video.

DEBRIEFING THE ELL SHADOWING EXPERIENCE

I left Josue's second period classroom knowing full well that he had not spent one minute in academic language production that day. I was frustrated and knew that something had to be done for Josue to graduate from high school and have some kind of future. Sadly, I also knew that there were many more students like Josue in this particular school system as well as across California and the country as a whole. In this way, the problem was systemic. Days like this were the very cause of the achievement gap. Unfortunately, we do not systemically and coherently train teachers to meet the specific needs of Josue and thousands of students like him. As the literature suggests, we do not currently provide teachers with enough training to become effective with our neediest groups of students. How do we expect to get different results when we know that teachers need coherent and aligned professional development in order to improve their own skills and student learning?

One way of aligning systems and creating urgency around the needs of this group of students comes through the ELL Shadowing Project previously described with Josue. Leaders of systems and those who work within them do not often have the time to take a look at the needs and instructional experiences of one student. ELL shadowing forces us to look at the specific needs of one student and reflect on how the things we do and don't do every day, either positively or negatively, impact that student's instructional progress. It reminds us that Josue does not have time to waste working independently on a worksheet unless the activity has been carefully designed for him. It forces us to realize that Josue must have ample opportunities to produce oral academic language in a classroom setting in order to become proficient in that language. Once they have shadowed an ELL, several educators have said things like "Once I got back into the classroom [after shadowing], I immediately changed around my instruction to create more classroom talk," and "The person talking the most is learning the most, and I'm doing the most talking!" (personal communication, Soto, 2003 and 2006).

It is important to remember, however, that ELL shadowing is not a silver bullet; it is not a canned program. It alone will not revolutionize your school or district—ELL shadowing is only the beginning of the conversation and exploration around the needs of ELLs, but it *can* be a catalyst to propel the work forward. ELL shadowing creates the urgency that must be in place to bring about true change. It provides the self-reflection that teachers and systems do not often have the luxury of doing. ELL shadowing must be followed up with focused, coherent, and sustained professional development over time. This follow-up professional development should then be focused on what was not seen surrounding specific ELL needs in the classroom setting. For example, since Josue needed more academic speaking to be embedded in both his Algebra I and biology classrooms, professional development should be targeted there. Josue needed to be *required* to speak and actively listen in both classrooms—only in these ways would he make meaning around the content. By keeping Josue's school experience in mind, both ELL shadowing and follow-up professional development can assist systems in changing practice. Educators no longer need to be convinced of the needs; they have now seen them before their very eyes, and it becomes difficult to turn away or teach in the same old way again.

REFERENCES

Fix, M., Mc Hugh, M., Terrazas, A., & Laglagaron, L. (2008). *Los Angeles on the leading edge: Immigrant integration indicators and their policy implications.* Washington, DC: Migration Policy Institute.

Soto-Hinman, I., & Hetzel, J. (2009). *The literacy gaps: Building bridges for English language learners and Standard English learners.* Thousand Oaks, CA: Corwin.

Tomas Rivera Policy Institute. (2009). *¿Qué pasa? Are English language learning students remaining in English learning classes too long?* Los Angeles, CA: Author.

Wei, R. C., Darling-Hammond, L., Andree, A., Richardson, N., & Orphanos, S. (2009). *Professional learning in the learning profession: A status report on teacher development in the United States and abroad.* Dallas, TX: National Staff Development Council.

SECTION II
Research Base

4

The Role of Academic Oral Language Development

The role of academic oral language development has become increasingly important for English Language Learners (ELLs) in a classroom setting. The National Literacy Panel (August & Shanahan, 2006), Goldenberg (2006), and Kinsella (2007) have also shed light on the importance of academic oral language on literacy development with ELLs. Specifically, August and Shanahan report an important finding that the foundation of literacy for ELLs is academic oral language practice. That is, ELLs must be given ample opportunities to use extended stretches of language, in order to become proficient academically in reading and writing in English. Goldenberg (2006) also suggests that "opportunities to extend oral English skills are critical for ELL students" (p. 35). Similarly, Kinsella (2007) recognizes that an essential element of academic language itself is the explicit teaching of the register of academic oral language itself, which includes teaching the distinctions between social—basic vocabulary, grammar, and form and function of language—and academic—content area vocabulary and syntax in context to reading and writing—language. It is also important to note that there are several components to academic language development, according to Kinsella (2007), including vocabulary development, syntax, grammar, and register. This definition of academic language will be used and addressed throughout the book, but only academic oral language development will be addressed in this chapter, for the purposes of preparing educators for the ELL shadowing experience.

Unfortunately, historically we have believed that quiet classrooms are good classrooms. We have thought that rows of students who compliantly listen while the teacher imparts knowledge into empty receptacles are best practice. Instead, what we must develop in a classroom setting is a culture of talking often about academic topics. We must find the language in the curriculum and elicit the voices in our classrooms. Even the best of instructional materials or programs may not emphasize the importance of academic oral language development in a classroom setting. This infusion of language must be done by educators via specific techniques and structures which *require* classroom talk (see Chapter 10 for specific techniques). This means that administrators within systems must give teachers the time and support to reinfuse academic oral language development into instructional materials. In this way, administrators and teachers alike should not expect or desire silence when they walk into classrooms. In order to create more academic oral language classroom settings, teachers must also be given the time to work in teams, by department or by grade level, in order to develop meaningful academic oral language development tasks. There must be a commitment to academic oral language development by everyone in the system in order for ELLs to be successful throughout their schooling experiences.

TEACHER-GUIDED REPORTING

ELLs are often relegated to Initiation-Response-Feedback (IRF) structures, whereby the students actually do very little talking (Gibbons, 2002). IRF is a process by which the teacher begins a conversation with a closed-ended question, such as "What color is the sky?" Such closed-ended questions require only a one- or two-word response and do not allow students to extend their discourse, vocabulary, or language sets. In this kind of exchange, the teacher usually ends such a conversation with "good job," and the conversation is considered over. Instead, Gibbons (2002), who has published widely on English language education, suggests an oral/academic language development structure called Teacher-Guided Reporting (TGR) whereby the teacher and student together construct what the ELL cannot say on his or her own. This includes several oral language scaffolds in order to encourage ELLs to use and extend language.

- **Open-ended questions**—In contrast to closed-ended questions, which require only a one-word response, open-ended questions extend language because there are multiple entryways and more than one way to formulate a response. An example of an open-ended question would be, "What do you notice about the sky?" This question could be answered in a variety of ways and requires more descriptive language, as well as longer stretches of language. When open-ended questions are used as a language scaffold, ELLs benefit greatly, as they get to extend their academic oral language repertoire. This strategy can also be used on its own, or with the entire scaffolding technique of TGR.

- **Clarification**—After posing an open-ended question, teachers should ask for clarification of language, including more descriptive or specific language, or a particular grammatical structure. For example, if a student answers that he notices that the sky is blue, the teacher can follow up with "What shade of blue?" or "What do you like about the sky?" The teacher may also require the student to complete the response using a language stem, such as "I noticed that the sky is light blue with hints of white clouds." If students cannot produce such language on their own due to their level of language proficiency, language stems such as "I noticed that the sky is _____ and _____" can be used. Such language stems should also grow and change as the school year progresses and as the ELL's language proficiency develops. More language stems have been included in the Academic Language Development Resources in Appendix B.

- **Encouragement**—When learning a second language, encouragement is helpful so that students are more likely to take language risks. When students panic or are not comfortable, they are more likely to shut down or not be willing to share responses publicly. Authentic encouraging responses such as "You're doing fine" and "Keep going" should be used with students often so that they are comfortable with taking language risks. Additionally, teachers should be sure to create a culture of language safety in the classroom setting. That is, students should not be allowed to make fun of each other for errors or language inversions.

- **Recasting**—Students are also more likely to shut down and oftentimes do not want to practice language when they are overly corrected or put on the spot for a language mistake. Instead, recasting is a strategy by which a student's response is restated in academic terms. For example, if a student says, "I want that troca," the teacher can recast, "You want that truck." This language correction does not put the student on the spot but also does not allow the error to go unnoticed. The teacher can then follow up with having the student repeat the sentence with the correct vocabulary embedded. Historically, when students have made language errors, teachers have either left such errors unaddressed or inappropriately and overly corrected students. This process of recasting ensures that errors are dealt with appropriately. ELLs are neither let "off the hook" nor are they shamed for language inversions.

GRAPHIC ORGANIZER FOR TEACHER-GUIDED REPORTING

The Graphic Organizer for TGR included in this chapter is a way for teachers to internalize and plan for all four steps in the TGR process.

Figure 4.1   Teacher-Guided Reporting Organizer

Objective: _____

Content Scenario: _____

_____

Language Scenario: _____

_____

Open-Ended Question *(multiple entry points/ no one-word responses)*	**Clarifying Questions** *(linguistic, more detail, complete sentences)*
Encouragement *(taking language risks)*	**Recasting** *(restating in academic language)*

Source: Adapted from Gibbons (2002).

Notice that teachers are first encouraged to "think through" the objective of the lesson, which is often associated with the academic content standards being addressed. Teachers should then think about the content and language scenarios in which they would like to use TGR. For example, TGR should not be used "cold" in a classroom setting. Rather, ELLs should have some recent and common academic experience, whereby they have developed some background knowledge, in order to have an academic conversation. Once teachers have internalized this process, they can then use all four steps—either together or independently—in a classroom setting to create more academic dialogue about recent topics. Figure 4.1 on page 25 is the TGR Graphic Organizer, also included in Appendix B, page 134.

BENEFITS OF LANGUAGE TALK FOR ELLS

Not all classroom talk is good talk, or the kind of academic oral language development that we want to occur in a classroom setting, but there are definite ways that ELLs benefit from language opportunities in a classroom setting. Specifically, according to Gibbons (2002) in *Scaffolding Language, Scaffolding Content*, ELLs benefit from language opportunities in the following ways:

- **Hear more language**—When ELLs talk to each other, they hear more language from a variety of sources. Instead of just hearing a message from the teacher, ELLs benefit from message redundancy and message abundancy, that is, hearing the message several times and in several different ways. The teacher should not be the only language model in the classroom setting. Students, especially when paired or grouped appropriately (high with low), can become language models for each other.
- **Practice more language**—ELLs oftentimes go home to communities where another language is spoken, or where another variation of English is spoken, for example, Chicano English or Hawaiian Pidgin. Therefore, ELLs benefit from as many structured opportunities to talk to each other and the teacher as possible. Such language exchanges must be planned in advance in order for it to actually occur. Teachers must find those places in the curriculum for specific language moments.
- **More comfortable about speaking**—ELLs are more likely to take language risks with each other rather than in a whole group setting. When students interact with each other in a structured format, they are more likely to take additional language turns. Structuring and modeling productive academic language, however, is the goal—so that students practice the appropriate kind of language needed, and so that teachers do not become frustrated by inappropriate language usage. Figure 4.2 summarizes the benefits of productive group work for ELLs (see Chapter 2).

Figure 4.2 Summary of Productive Group Work for ELLs

1. They hear more language.	
2. They speak more language.	
3. They understand more language.	
4. They ask more questions.	
5. They are more comfortable about speaking.	

Source: Gibbons (2002), pp. 230–231.

Despite the many language benefits suggested by Gibbons (2002), teachers may still be wary of allowing talk in the classroom for fear of management issues, or that the wrong kinds of conversations may ensue. It is important to note that classroom talk must be modeled and practiced before movement into independent practice. Specific ways to set up academic oral language development will be explored in Chapter 10.

ELLs also benefit from productive group work, but not all group work is effective or productive. Unfortunately, many educators recall poor experiences with group work structures, where they perhaps did most of the work for the group, or not much work got done at all. These poor models were not effective and productive group work. For group work to be productive, it must be modeled and practiced as a whole class before students are expected to independently engage in group work themselves. According to Gibbons (2002), eight characteristics of Productive Group Work must be taught explicitly for group work to be effective so that it can then elicit more academic talk in the classroom setting:

1. **Clear and explicit instructions are provided.** Students, especially ELLs, must know what is expected of them before they are expected

to complete a task. From classroom noise levels, to assignment details and time limits—all of these expectations must be made clear and modeled in order for students to be successful in the classroom. This means that teachers must have thought through each of these details before a group work structure is utilized. For example, if a teacher is going to have a group of four for a group work structure, how will she keep each student on task and accountable? How long will it take to complete the task? How will each student role be assessed? Will there be both group and individual accountability? More about each of these components will be explored in Chapter 10, after ELL shadowing has been completed.

2. **Talk is necessary for the task.** When educators place students in groups, they must *require* student talk. The kind of talk—academic in nature—must be carefully designed, but we should not put students into groups and then expect them to be silent. In fact, the assignments within those groups should organize the talking task so that it is both academic in nature and productive. Again, planning for necessary talk that is both structured and productive is essential to group work tasks. Each student in the group should be held responsible for academic talk with a specific task and accountability for language. This can be done by providing language stems that can be used with each specific group role (examples of this can be found in Chapter 10).

3. **There is a clear outcome.** ELLs must know that they will be held accountable for group work tasks. This means that each student should have a specific role that is appropriately tailored to the standards and objectives associated with the assignment. Additionally, the task should be linguistically and cognitively appropriate so that student progress can be monitored. For example, if a student is a beginning level English speaker, he or she should be provided with additional language and content scaffolds in order to be successful with the assignment. This may mean providing the student with both language stems for academic language practice (see Appendix B), as well as a word wall for vocabulary development within the content area. ELLs at higher levels of English language development may need more sophisticated language stems that demonstrate how to have academic conversations, as well as vocabulary word walls to be successful with academic vocabulary. Determining each ELL's specific language need is helpful with this process.

4. **The task is cognitively appropriate.** Group work tasks should not be too simple or too difficult to be completed within a group setting. This notion fits well with Vygotsky's (1986) 1936 Zone of Proximal Development (ZPD) or the gap between what a learner can do with or without additional assistance or scaffolding. A student should work in groups when a particular task is just too difficult to be completed on one's own. That is, there should be

cognitive challenge associated with the talk. Additionally, group work can be assigned when the teacher determines that a particular skill or concept takes multiple repetitions to fully internalize. For ELLs to benefit from group work, the tasks should be talking oriented, causing students to make deeper meaning by using academic language to work through key concepts. The task should also lend itself to working together, in order for there to be success with the task.

5. **The task is integrated with a broader topic.** Group work tasks should integrate academic and linguistic objectives. That is, group work structures that promote academic language should not be taught outside of the content. For example, after students read already required text selections, they can complete reciprocal teaching roles, in order to keep them on task and accountable. This sort of exercise combines both group work and content. It also allows educators to amplify the academic oral language development oftentimes taken out of the curriculum. By having students talk about and not merely read texts, they will make deeper meaning around the content and also practice language. Procedures for how to set up reciprocal teaching are introduced in Chapter 10, as a way to systemically elicit more academic oral language development after ELL shadowing has been completed.

6. **All children are involved.** Each ELL should be held accountable for both academic oral language development in groups and an individual academic task so that comprehension can be monitored. If each student in a group does not have a task or role, he or she is less likely to practice language and benefit from the group work interaction. Additionally, each student should be given multiple academic oral language development stems so that he or she understands how to participate in academic discourse.

7. **Students have enough time.** ELLs should be given enough time to complete tasks. If students are given too much time, they are off-task. If they have too little time, they are more likely to get frustrated. When teachers plan for a particular assignment or activity, they should estimate the amount of time students need to complete tasks. Teachers can then use timers to monitor student activity, as well as to ensure that they are not losing precious instructional time. I typically start students off with an initial amount of time—somewhere between ten and twenty minutes, depending on the task—and then adjust the time depending on how students are progressing. It is essential that the teacher monitor group work by walking around the room, in order to determine how much additional time students may need to be successful with a task or assignment.

8. **Students know how to work in groups.** It is important for educators to utilize the gradual release of responsibility to independent practice,

in order for students to be successful with group work. That is, teachers should never expect students to be able to complete a task on their own without ample modeling. One way to do this is to use the fishbowl approach, whereby a pair or group of students comes to the front of the classroom, and they model what effective Pair-Share or group conversations look like. The teacher should work with students who will model ahead of time, in order to ensure that appropriate modeling is provided. Providing this level of scaffolding will allow students to be successful with group work. Teachers will also be less frustrated with issues when they arise. Although modeling takes time at the beginning, it ensures that fewer problems occur in the end for both the teacher and the student. Figure 4.3 is a summary of the characteristics of effective group work described previously.

Figure 4.3 Characteristics of Effective Group Work for ELLs

1. Clear and explicit instructions are provided.	5. The task is integrated with a broader topic.
2. Talk is necessary for the task.	6. All children are involved.
3. There is a clear outcome.	7. Students have enough time.
4. The task is cognitively appropriate.	8. Students know how to work in groups.

Source: Gibbons (2002), pp. 20–28.

MONITORING ACADEMIC ORAL LANGUAGE DEVELOPMENT DURING ELL SHADOWING

According to August and Shanahan (2002), since ELLs spend less than 2 percent of their school day in academic oral language development, it is an eye-opening and self-reflective experience for educators to monitor academic speaking specifically over the course of two hours of ELL shadowing. Only after educators have understood the literature and the importance of academic oral language development in a classroom setting are they ready to monitor academic speaking in a classroom setting. Once educators have been provided with a profile of the ELL, they will shadow for two hours (this will be provided by training organizers; see Chapter 6) and begin tracking his or her academic oral language development at every five-minute interval (at least two hours is the recommended time when shadowing). It is important that participants understand that they are monitoring the primary situation that is occurring at the top of the five-minute interval and not for the entire five-minute interval itself. For example, if an ELL begins the top of the five-minute interval by writing, but in that same five-minute interval turns and talks to a partner, only the writing activity should be monitored. This is important for interrater reliability reasons—that is, so that everyone is using the same structure and procedure when monitoring their ELL. Additionally, it is important to note that the purpose of shadowing is to explore a day in the life of an ELL. The process is not a running record but a way to gather general trends and patterns in academic oral language development and active listening for ELLs within a school system. Similarly, in order to ensure interrater reliability, educators should also use the codes shown in Figure 4.4 for every five-minute interval being monitored.

Figure 4.4 ELL Shadowing Codes

Primary Speaker	Mostly to Whom?	Primary Speaker	Mostly to Whom?	
Your Student	1. Student	**Teacher**	5. Student	**SPEAKING**
	2. Teacher		6. Small Group	
	3. Small Group		7. Whole class	
	4. Whole Class			

ELL SHADOWING CODES FOR ACADEMIC SPEAKING

The codes above will be checked off on the ELL Shadowing Protocol form (see Figure 4.5 for speaking). The purpose is to monitor, at the top of every five-minute interval, what the primary speaker—either the ELL or teacher—is doing in terms of academic speaking. Again, it is important to remember that whatever is occurring at the *top* of the five-minute interval is what should be monitored. The ELL shadowing form is not a running record, whereby everything within that time period is written down. Instead, educators should only take down what is happening *most* at the beginning of that five-minute time frame so that general trends and patterns can be discussed within a system. Figure 4.5 is a blank of the academic speaking section of the ELL Shadowing Protocol Form (for the full form, see Figure 7.3 on page 65; Appendix A, page 119; or http://www .corwin.com/ellshadowing).

Although the purpose of ELL shadowing is to monitor the ELL's academic speaking and listening, there will be times when the student is not

Figure 4.5 Blank Academic Speaking Section

Academic Speaking (check one)	Comments
❏ Student to Student—1	
❏ Student to Teacher—2	
❏ Student to Small Group—3	
❏ Student to Whole Class—4	
❏ Teacher to Student—5	
❏ Teacher to Small Group—6	
❏ Teacher to Whole Class—7	

the primary speaker because the teacher is talking. Therefore, there are two sets of codes, one for students and one for the teacher. When the student is speaking, Codes 1 through 4 should be checked off. When the teacher is talking, Codes 5 through 7 should be checked off. For example, if the ELL student is speaking to a partner then Box 1 should be checked off as noted in Figure 4.6. The process of coding specific academic speaking modes over a two-hour period allows educators to see firsthand the lack of academic oral language development opportunities experienced by ELLs in a classroom setting. When groups of educators complete this project, we begin to see how this relative silence begins to negatively impact instruction for ELLs.

Figure 4.6   Academic Speaking Coded for ELL

Academic Speaking (check one)	Comments
☑ Student to Student—1	
☐ Student to Teacher—2	
☐ Student to Small Group—3	
☐ Student to Whole Class—4	
☐ Teacher to Student—5	
☐ Teacher to Small Group—6	
☐ Teacher to Whole Class—7	

However, if the teacher is speaking to the whole class, then Box 7 should be checked off as noted in Figure 4.7.

Figure 4.7   Academic Speaking Coded for Teacher

Academic Speaking (check one)	Comments
☐ Student to Student—1	
☐ Student to Teacher—2	
☐ Student to Small Group—3	
☐ Student to Whole Class—4	
☐ Teacher to Student—5	
☐ Teacher to Small Group—6	
☑ Teacher to Whole Class—7	

Comments Section of ELL Shadowing Protocol Form

In addition to the left-hand side of the shadowing observation form, there is also the comments section on the right-hand side of the form. This is a place where qualitative information, which cannot be captured merely by checking off a box, should be recorded. For example, if the teacher is talking, but the student is struggling or not fully listening, this is the place where that information can be taken down. If the student is confused, or something unusual is noticed, it can be written here. Additionally, this section is the place to write whatever happens beyond the top of the first five-minute interval. That is, if at the start of the interval, the ELL is on task and working on his or her assignment, but within the same five-minute interval is off-task, then the on-task behavior should be checked off, but the off-task behavior can be documented in the comments section. Positive comments can also be noted here, as well as comments that are about the teacher and not the student.

Figure 4.8 is an example of the kind of comments that you might record when shadowing your ELL student.

Figure 4.8   Comments Section of ELL Shadowing Protocol Form

Comments
Josue started this five-minute interval by being on task with his quick write. He seemed to be really engaged and interested in the topic at first. Unfortunately, he quickly got off task and started talking to the person next to him. He seemed to struggle a bit with writing anything more than a couple of sentences.

The comments section of the ELL shadow observation form provides useful information during the debriefing session, so it is important to take down careful notes that will allow patterns and themes from the observation to emerge. In the debriefing portion of the ELL shadowing training, educators will be asked to summarize their comments into a few sentences on a sticky note. From there, themes and patterns from all of the comments will assist with triangulating the classroom data that was coded for the academic speaking portion of the ELL Shadowing Protocol Form (this is described further in Chapter 7).

REFERENCES

August, D., & Shanahan, T. (2006). *Developing literacy in second-language learners: Report of the national literacy panel on language minority children and youth.* Mahwah, NJ: Erlbaum.

Gibbons, P. (2002). *Scaffolding language, scaffolding learning: Teaching second language learners in the mainstream classroom*. Portsmouth, NH: Heinemann.

Goldenberg, C. (2006, July 26). Improving achievement for English learners: What the research tells us. *Education Week*, pp. 34–36.

Kinsella, K. (2007). *Bolstering academic language and reading comprehension*. PowerPoint presentation at the Academic Language Development Workshop, Mountain View School, El Monte, CA. Available at http://www.sccoe.k12.ca.us/depts/ell/kinsella_2009.asp

Vygotsky, L. S. (1986). *Thought and language* (Rev. ed.). Cambridge, MA: MIT Press.

5

The Importance of Active Listening

Listening, like speaking, is an underdeveloped domain in most classrooms (Gibbons, 2002). Historically, we have overly emphasized reading and writing as the heavy-hitting domains that will be tested, making them somehow academically more important. We also often assume that students know how to listen, and we do not take the time to explicitly teach students how to do so—until, of course, students are off-task and we become increasingly frustrated with them. In teacher education programs, unfortunately, preservice teachers are often not taught how to embed and plan for listening in their lesson planning. For English Language Learners (ELLs), however, learning how to actively listen and being required to do so becomes an important learning scaffold. In this way, listening is connected to reading, just as speaking is a scaffold for writing. Listening and reading are both about taking in information, or making meaning from sounds or text. Spending time teaching your students, especially your ELLs, to listen is not in vain. It is a lifelong skill that will assist them. Additionally, when we assist students with the ways in which they can listen, we provide support and reinforcement for the ways in which they can read—either specifically or generally.

NUNAN'S QUADRANTS OF LISTENING

For example, Nunan (1990) suggests that there are two contexts for listening—academic and social—with academic listening being the most difficult of the two, therefore requiring the most scaffolding or support. He also suggests that we can listen in two ways: (1) one-way listening, whereby we take in information without being able to clarify or ask questions, as in a lecture, and (2) two-way listening, whereby there is a dialogue of some sort and students can be supported with questions and clarification. Figure 5.1 is a visual of Nunan's Quadrants of Listening, with examples of what happens in each kind of context (interpersonal/social vs. information based/academic).

Figure 5.1 Nunan's Quadrants of Listening With Modified Example

	Two-way listening (dialogue)		
Interpersonal (social) topics	**Quadrant A** *Taking part in* • Conversation at a party • Conversation at a bus stop about the weather • A chatty phone call to a friend	**Quadrant C** *Taking part in* • A job interview • A conversation involving giving directions or instructions • A phone inquiry about buying a computer	Information based (academic)
	Quadrant B *Listening to* • Someone recounting a personal anecdote • Someone telling a story • Someone telling a joke	**Quadrant D** *Listening to* • The radio or TV news • A lecture • Phone information (e.g., instructions for paying a bill)	
	One-way (lecture)		

Source: Adapted from Nunan, D. (1990).

When shadowing an ELL, educators are asked to monitor the kinds of listening that students are required to participate in within a classroom setting, at every five-minute interval as per Nunan's Quadrants of Listening. Educators then check off the appropriate section for listening, much like it is described in the academic speaking chapter.

CODING FOR ACADEMIC LISTENING

Figure 5.2 is a blank listening form to be used during ELL shadowing. Notice that there are two sections to the academic listening portion of the protocol. On the left-hand side, there is a section for monitoring academic listening, either one way (lecture) or two way (dialogue or conversation). The section on the right asks educators to monitor whether the ELL is not required to listen or not listening at all.

Figure 5.2 Blank Listening Form

Academic Listening: One-Way or Two-Way (check one)	Student Is Not Listening (check one)

☐ Student listening mostly to student—1
 	
☐ Student listening mostly to teacher—2
 	
☐ Student listening mostly to
   small group—3
 	
☐ Student listening mostly to
   whole class—4
 	
NOTE: One-way (lecture) or two-way (dialogue)
	☐ Reading or writing silently—1
	
	☐ Student is off-task—2

As they did with the academic speaking section of the ELL shadowing form, educators should code listening behaviors at the top of every five-minute interval. Notice on the left-hand side of the ELL shadowing form that educators are only asked to monitor student listening. Unlike the academic speaking portion, there is no section to monitor teacher listening levels, so there are only four options to check off as noted in the Academic Listening Codes section that follows. Notice that there is an additional section for academic listening to be used when students are not listening. This can be coded in two different ways: (1) reading or writing silently, which does not require active listening; (2) student is off-task and should have been listening.

Academic Listening Codes

Figure 5.3 shows the ELL shadowing codes for academic listening, which are to be used when monitoring ELL listening behaviors only.

Figure 5.3 Shadowing Codes

Listening	
Primary Listener	**Listening Mostly to Whom?**
Your Student	1. Student
	2. Teacher
	3. Small group
	4. Whole class

Source: Soto-Hinman (2010).

As demonstrated in the coding system, academic listening will be monitored as follows:

- A student listening mostly to another student, as during a Think-Pair-Share
- A student listening mostly to the teacher, as during a lecture or individual conference
- A student listening mostly to a small group, as in a group experiment or productive group work
- A student listening mostly to the whole class, as during a choral reading or singing

These four codes will allow educators to efficiently monitor the academic listening opportunities that ELLs are engaged in during a school day.

Academic Listening (One Way or Two Way)

In Figure 5.4, the listening portion of the ELL shadowing form has been coded as a 2 because the student was listening to the teacher during a science

Figure 5.4 Completed Form for Academic Listening

Academic Listening One-Way or Two-Way (check one)
One-way (lecture) or two-way (dialogue)
☐ Student listening mostly to student—1
☑ Student listening mostly to teacher—2
☐ Student listening mostly to small group—3
☐ Student listening mostly to whole class—4

demonstration. At the start of the five-minute interval, the teacher demonstrated the use of a beaker to transfer liquid from a bottle to a petri dish. The entire class, including the ELL, watched the teacher modeling this and the next steps for an experiment before students were separated into small groups to complete their own experiments.

During the teacher modeling of the lab experiment described previously, the ELL actively listened and took notes on a graphic organizer provided by the teacher on how to replicate the experiment in the groups. Because the student was on task and actively taking notes, the second box of the academic listening section was checked off.

Not Listening or Not Required to Listen

The middle section of the ELL shadowing form requires educators to monitor when students are not listening or are not required to listen. Figure 5.5 is a blank ELL shadowing form to be used only when students are demonstrating one of these two behaviors.

Figure 5.5   Completed Form for Student Not Listening

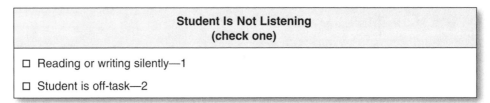

Student Is Not Listening **(check one)**
☐ Reading or writing silently—1
☐ Student is off-task—2

When ELLs are not required to listen, as in reading or writing silently, their responses are coded in the far-right column as 1. When students are off-task and are supposed to be listening but are not, the response is coded as a 2. During the debriefing session, all of these codes will be added up so that themes and patterns can be determined for the group of ELLs shadowed at a particular school site.

Figure 5.6 is a shadowing form that has been coded a 1 because the ELL was completing an independent quickwrite assignment at the beginning of class. The student was on task and writing to the prompt, so the first box was checked off.

Figure 5.6   Completed Academic Listening Form

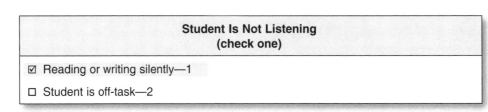

Student Is Not Listening **(check one)**
☑ Reading or writing silently—1
☐ Student is off-task—2

More description on how to use the ELL shadowing protocol and how to code listening and speaking specifically can be found in Chapter 7.

REFERENCES

Nunan, D. (1990). Learning to listen in a second language. *Prospect, 5*(2), 7–23. Available at http://www.ameprc.mq.edu.au/resources/prospect/V5_N2_1990

Olsen, L. (2010). *Reparable harm: Fulfilling the unkept promise of educational opportunity for California's long term English learners.* Long Beach, CA: Californians Together. Available at http://www.californianstogether.org/

SECTION III

Preparation for Shadowing

6

Preparing for a Shadowing Training

ORGANIZING AND SETTING UP A SHADOWING PROJECT

The following section describes what is needed to begin to organize an English Language Learner (ELL) shadowing training. It is important to note that the ELL shadowing training includes two parts, segmented into two days, as follows:

Day 1: Preparation for Training

AM: Background research and training on listening and speaking

PM: Training on how to use the ELL shadowing protocol and directions for Day 2

Day 2: ELL Shadowing and Debriefing

AM: ELL Shadowing at school sites

PM: Debriefing the shadowing experience

Obtaining ELL Achievement Data for Planning

In order for an ELL shadowing training to be successful, the organizers of the training must determine what English language development level, or kind of ELL, they would like their participants to shadow. For example, if many ELLs within a system are not making progress at the midway point in English language development, which is often common, then educators may choose to shadow ELLs at that level. If most ELLs within a system remain at the final levels of English language proficiency without becoming fluent in English, then participants should shadow there. Or if there are many newcomers in a particular system and there is a desire to target their needs, then shadowing commences here. In this way, each ELL shadowing training should be tailored to the specific needs of the particular students who are struggling within that system. Having a group or committee that can analyze ELL data within the system, in order to make the most change and have the most effect ahead of time, is optimal. For example, in Lucia Mar Unified School District in Arroyo Grande, California, the ELL teacher on special assignment (TOSA) worked with schools to collect student data from the centralized data system and to organize the specifics of the training. This also alleviated the school site from an additional assignment, since the school would be hosting the event.

DISTRICTWIDE ELL SHADOWING

When organizing a districtwide ELL shadowing training, it is important for district organizers to backward map the agenda, details, and information that will be needed. First, organizers will need to determine how many shadowing participants they will have in a particular training. The more participants that are included, the more ELL profiles will be needed for those participants to shadow on Day 2 of the training, which can also cause more of an impact at the school site. Once the numbers are determined, organizers will need to contact schools, often at the elementary, middle, and high school levels, to gain permission to shadow at those sites. For example, in Norwalk–La Mirada Unified School District in Norwalk, California, all administrators participated in ELL shadowing according to school level. Elementary school administrators shadowed ELLs on one day, middle school administrators on another day, and high school administrators on still another day. When each administrator had shadowed an ELL, everyone was called together for the debriefing session and for planning the next steps. Each of these days was a half-day session in order to reduce the amount of time that administrators were away from their school sites. Figure 6.1 is a sample agenda from the ELL shadowing trainings in the Norwalk–La Mirada Unified School District.

Figure 6.1 ELL Shadowing Agenda for Day 1

Norwalk–La Mirada Unified School District
Day 1 ELL SHADOWING TRAINING
October 1, 2010

AGENDA

8:00—Welcome and Agenda Review

8:15—Oral/Academic Language Development Overview

10:00—Break

10:30—Listening Overview

Shadowing Introduction/Practice With the Protocol Day 2 Agenda Overview/
Logistics/Student Profiles

12:00—Closing

PLEASE DON'T FORGET TO WEAR YOUR

DISTRICT ID TO THE OBSERVATION SCHOOL ON DAY 2.

Similarly, in the Lucia-Mar Unified School District in Arroyo Grande, California, ninety administrators, teachers, and district office staff members participated in a two-day ELL shadowing experience, according to school level. After being trained on how to shadow on Day 1, each teacher and administrator was assigned to an ELL at an elementary, middle, or high school within the district and shadowed that student on Day 2. Many individual schools within Lucia-Mar Unified School District have now shadowed ELLs at their specific school sites so that more teachers could have the experience of shadowing.

As has been explained in previous chapters, ELL shadowing begins with training on the importance of academic speaking and listening for ELLs. This overview provides the grounding and ensures that everyone who is shadowing has the same lens by which to go into classrooms. Figure 6.2 is the agenda for Day 2 of the ELL shadowing training in the Norwalk–La Mirada Unified School District.

Note that the agenda for Day 2 includes details such as the premeeting time and meeting location. The premeeting location is where participants will meet at the school site before the actual shadowing occurs in classrooms. This brief time period allows the organizers to review the expectations and directions for shadowing that day. Additionally, during this time period, the ELL student profile will be distributed (for the full form, see Figure 6.5 on page 51; Appendix A, page 125; or http://www.corwin.com/ellshadowing). The ELL student profile includes the student's schedule, room number, and language development level, as well as achievement data (a sample student profile is included on page 53). Typically, a school site representative will be present to assist with room number distributions and a map of the school.

Figure 6.2 ELL Shadowing Agenda for Day 2

Norwalk–La Mirada Unified School District
Day 2 ELL SHADOWING TRAINING
AGENDA

School Site Visit Information

Johnston Elementary School (October 8, 2010)

Meeting Room: G-2
Premeeting Time: 7:45 am

Los Alisos Middle School (October 22, 2010)

Meeting Room: 104
Premeeting Time: 7:30 am

John Glenn High School (October 29, 2010)

Meeting Room: Library
Premeeting Time: 7:50 am

8:00–10:00 AM—ELL Shadowing

10:00 AM—Break/Recess

10:25 AM—Shadowing Debrief

11:15 AM—Wrap, Evaluations, PD Survey, Next Steps

Some additional reminders to participants during the premeeting are included in Figure 6.3.

Figure 6.3 Do's and Don'ts of Shadowing

- Do shadow at the school level of your assignment.
- Do help become familiar with forms.
- Do help maintain focus on the student.

- Don't ask for a boutique assignment.
- Don't ask student any formal questions.
- Don't share any evaluative statements about teacher or class.

Source: Adapted from Gibbons (2002).

Do's and Don'ts of Shadowing

It is important for participants to shadow at the same level at which they teach or are administrators. This is important especially the first time that ELL shadowing is done so participants can be more reflective about their own specific settings and practices. If classrooms or schools are not similar to what educators encounter every day, it may be more difficult to leverage change from the experience because the students or community are so different. In the afternoon of Day 1 of the ELL shadowing training, participants are taught how to use the ELL shadowing protocol, much as it is described in Chapters 4 and 5. Participants should be reminded at the end of Day 1 that they should bring the sample protocol with them on Day 2 of the training. Additionally, training organizers should make enough copies of the ELL shadowing protocol, which often means three back-to-back copies so that participants can shadow their ELLs for two full hours (see blank copy in Appendix A, page 119). Organizers should review how to fill out the form during the preplanning portion of the onsite training at the school. Participants should also be reminded that focus should be maintained on the student and not the teacher or other students. Student shadowing is about a day in the life of an ELL and not placing blame on any part of the system. Participants should be reminded that neither the student nor teacher should be aware of the ELL who is being shadowed so the data collection is not impacted. All teachers at a school site should be alerted that classroom observations of ELLs in general are occurring, but they should not be told the specific students who are being shadowed. Also, participants should be reminded not sit too close to their ELLs so that students do not become aware that they are being shadowed.

Don'ts of Shadowing

Participants should also be reminded of what should not occur during a shadowing observation both on the afternoon of Day 1 of the ELL shadowing training and at the premeeting on Day 2 of the training. Both organizers and participants should not ask teachers to provide a special or boutique lesson. Instead, teachers should do what they typically do when observers are not in the room. Organizers of the training should also tell teachers that participants will be in rooms to learn from ELLs, but they should not indicate which specific student will be observed. This will ensure that teachers will not act any differently than normal toward that student. In this same vein, specific evaluative statements about the class or student should not be shared with the teacher so as to reinforce that the observation was about the student and not the teacher or classroom (the change in teacher practices comes in the follow-up professional development). Finally, participants should not interact with the ELL or other students in class. Participants should try to be as unobtrusive as possible, including placing cell phones in vibrate mode. All of these suggestions will ensure that the ELL Shadowing training is as successful as possible.

Determining ELL Shadowing Numbers

Since each shadowing participant will need an ELL to shadow, it is important to determine training numbers early on. The organizers (district office staff members or school site administrators) will need to ensure that they have enough ELLs at corresponding school sites for those participants to shadow. For example, if a particular school site or school district has thirty participants at the elementary, middle, and high school levels at a particular training, it would need to make sure that it has at least one elementary, one middle, and one high school that is willing to host the shadowing event. Participants should shadow at the level of their daily work. Participants can also shadow in pairs in order to alleviate the impact on classrooms, but it is not recommended to have more than two observers in a classroom at one time, as it can be overwhelming for the teacher. Also, there often is not enough classroom space to comfortably house more than two observers in a room.

Selecting ELLs for Shadowing

Before the ELL shadowing event, it is also important to have organizers determine the English language proficiency level of need within the school or district so that information can be communicated to the school or district office when selecting students. If most ELLs are not making progress at the midrange of language ability, then shadowing should be done at that level of proficiency. If the district office can access school site ELL data, it is best to do that for each of the sites so that schools do not have one more task on their plates. Figure 6.4 is an ELL Student Profile for Shadowing Form (also included in Appendix A page 125, and at http://www.corwin.com/ellshadowing) that can be helpful as a guide regarding the demographic information and type of achievement data that will be needed for shadowing.

Figure 6.4 ELL Student Profile for Shadowing Form

- First Name
- Date of Birth
- Date of Entry in US
- Date of Entry in District

Test Results (last three years, if possible):

- Language Proficiency Assessment
- State Achievement Scores for ELA & Math
- Grades
- GPA
- High School Exit Exam Scores (HS only)

If the district office has access to the data for the school via a database, then it only needs to ask schools to provide a picture of each student to be shadowed. The picture is important so that shadowing participants can easily identify students in a classroom when observing. The first name of the student is important so that the shadowing participant can connect with the ELL as a human being. For privacy reasons, the last name of the student is not necessary. The date of birth and grade level is important so that the educator can compare the chronological age to the current grade level and English language development level that the student is in. All of this demographic information should be collected before a shadowing training and when determining final training capacity numbers. Figure 6.5, also included in Appendix A (page 125) and at http://www.corwin.com/ellshadowing, lists the demographic information needed for the ELL to be shadowed.

The dates of entry into the United States and into the district allow the educator to later analyze the level of progress that the student has made in terms of his or her English language proficiency. The goal in California is that ELLs should progress one language proficiency level per year; other states have determined their own Annual Measurable Academic Objective (AMAO). The English language proficiency levels or language assessment data (in California, this is the California English Language Development Test, or CELDT), is helpful for progress monitoring analysis and to make initial recommendations regarding student need. Figure 6.6 shows how the English language proficiency data should be collected for each ELL shadowed.

The state standardized or grade-level assessment data is helpful when monitoring annual grade-level academic progress (in California, this is the California Standards Test, or CST). An ELL's grades, grade point average (GPA), and additional assessment scores also provide eye-opening information, especially as this information can be triangulated with the observation once ELL shadowing is completed. The classroom periods, teachers, and room numbers are important so educators can find and follow (at the secondary level) their respective ELL from classroom to classroom when shadowing. Figure 6.7 includes the sections to be completed for the state achievement results, grades, GPA, and high school exit exam results.

The final section of the ELL shadowing profile is for the student's schedule so the educator knows where to find the ELL once he or she is at the school site. All of this information will be reviewed at the premeeting at the school on Day 2 of the shadowing training. Figure 6.8 is a completed ELL shadowing profile form that each participant will receive before shadowing an ELL on Day 2.

Figure 6.8 contains the necessary information to both successfully shadow an ELL and analyze the ELL's progress during the debriefing session. It will be further explained in the section that follows.

Figure 6.5 Blank ELL Student Profile for Shadowing

- Picture of ELL for visual identification
- First name
- Date of birth
- Grade level
- Date of entry into United States
- Date of entry into district

Test Results (last three years, if possible)

Classes or Periods to Be Shadowed

Period/Class	Course Title	Teacher	Room #

CELDT[a] Overall	Listening and Speaking	Reading	Writing

CST[b] for ELA[c] and Math	Grades	GPA	CAHSEE[d] (HS only)

a. California English Language Development Test.

b. California Standards Test.

c. English Language Arts.

d. California High School Exit Exam.

Figure 6.6 Language Development Results

Test Results (last three years, if possible)			
English Language Proficiency Overall	Listening and Speaking	Reading	Writing

Figure 6.7 State Assessment Results and Class Schedule

Classes or Periods to Be Shadowed

Period/Class	Course Title	Teacher	Room #

Test Results (last three years, if possible)

State Assessment for ELA[a] and Math	Grades	GPA	High School Exit Exam Results

a. English Language Arts.

Figure 6.8 Completed ELL Student Profile for Shadowing

- Picture of ELL for visual identification

- First Name: *Josue*
- Date of Birth: *8/94*
- Grade level: *10*
- Date of Entry in US: *9/99*
- Date of Entry in District: *9/99*

Classes or Periods to Be Shadowed:

Period/Class	Course Title	Teacher	Room #
1	English 10 P	Ms. Partridge	4A
2	Algebra 4	Mr. Gonzalez	113

Test Results (last three years, if possible)

English Language Proficiency (CELDT[a]) Scores Overall	Listening and Speaking	Reading	Writing
Fall 2007: 4	4, 4	5	4
Fall 2008: 4	4, 4	3	4
Fall 2009: 4	4, 3	3	4

Grade Level (CST[b]) Scores for ELA[c] and Math	Grades	GPA	CAHSEE[d] (HS only)
ELA: 331	ELA: B	Total: 2.9091	ELA: Passed
Math: 279	Math: C	Academic: 2.8000	Math: Passed

a. California English Language Development Test **Testing Key:** 5 (Advanced), 4 (Early Advanced), 3 (Intermediate), 2 (Early Intermediate), 1 (Beginning).

b. California Standards Test.

c. English Language Arts.

d. California High School Exit Exam.

DATA TALK FOR ELL SHADOWING DEBRIEFING

The ELL shadowing profile should also be analyzed again during the debriefing session of the ELL shadowing training in order to determine patterns and themes across all students and levels. The quantitative information—assessment data, grades, and GPA—can be compared against the qualitative data gathered via shadowing. Figure 6.9 shows the demographic information for Josue, along with a sample of the kind of analysis that should happen during the data talk portion of the debriefing session following the ELL shadowing experience.

Figure 6.9 Completed Demographic Information on ELL Student Profile for Shadowing

- Picture of ELL for visual identification

- First Name: *Josue*
- Date of Birth: *8/94*
- Grade level: *10*
- Date of Entry in US: *9/99*
- Date of Entry in District: *9/99*

According to the demographic data, Josue had been in the country for eleven years at the time of shadowing, with only four years of English language development progress. This makes Josue a Long-Term EL or LTEL, an ELL who has been in the country six years or more without reclassifying as fluent in English. The literature on LTELs tells us that Josue needs more academic literacy development, which will grow out of the opportunities that educators provide for his oral language development.

Figure 6.10 shows Josue's English language proficiency scores for the past three years. The scores in Figure 6.10 demonstrate that Josue has not made progress on his overall scores over the past three years. Scores have remained the same at 4, for the past three years. After eleven years in the country, Josue should have already reclassified as fluent in English, according to both California state expectations (one language level per year) and second language acquisition research (three to five years overall for the social/basics of English; five to seven years for academic English).

Figure 6.10   English Language Proficiency Scores

English Language Development (CELDT[a]) Scores Overall	Listening and Speaking	Reading	Writing
Fall 2007: 4	*4, 4*	*5*	*4*
Fall 2008: 4	*4, 4*	*3*	*4*
Fall 2009: 4	*4, 3*	*3*	*4*

a. California English Language Development Test.
Testing Key: 5 (Advanced), 4 (Early Advanced), 3 (Intermediate), 2 (Early Intermediate), 1 (Beginning).

Notice that Josue's listening scores have flatlined for the past three years and that he has regressed in speaking as he has moved from 4 to 3. Similarly, Josue has regressed in reading by moving back two scores from 2007 to 2008 and maintaining that level in 2009. Josue has also flatlined in terms of his writing scores. This data shows that after eleven years in the country, Josue needs more rigorous and structured academic oral language development opportunities, which can also lead to academic literacy development. More discussion on how to provide this kind of instruction will be discussed in Chapter 10.

Academic Achievement Scores

Regarding academic achievement, Josue demonstrated below grade-level assessment scores on the state assessment called the California Standards Test (CST), although he had passed the high school exit exam. The California High School Exit Exam (CAHSEE), however, only measures eighth grade math and English skills. So although it is a positive indicator that Josue has passed the CAHSEE, he still has much more progress to make in terms of grade-level expectations. This is evident by Josue's grades and overall grade point average. Although Josue was receiving a *B* in English at the time of shadowing, he was taking a sheltered English course for ELLs. In a couple of years, when Josue enters college or the workplace, he will need much more than just basic English courses to succeed in college and beyond.

Josue was also struggling in his Algebra 4 class with a grade of *C*. Algebra 4 means that Josue has taken Algebra I four different times. But Josue will need much more than Algebra I to be considered for most jobs in the 21st century. The notion that an eleventh grader is taking such courses at all is a systemic issue that must be addressed by educational institutions as a whole. Olsen, in *Reparable Harm* (2010), suggests that ELLs who have been in the country six years or more and are not making progress, as Josue is not, need specialized courses that will accelerate instruction while also teaching English, not further watering down of content.

Such issues will be explored further in the debriefing section of the book. Figure 6.11 shows Josue's academic progress in English Language Arts (ELA) and Mathematics.

Figure 6.11 ELL Achievement Data

Grade Level CST[a] Scores for ELA and Math	Grades	GPA	CAHSEE[b] (HS only)
ELA: 331	ELA: B	Total: 2.9091	ELA: Passed
Math: 279	Math: C	Academic: 2.8000	Math: Passed

a. California Standards Test.
b. California High School Exit Exam.

As shown in Figure 6.11, Josue's GPA is just below a C average at 2.80, which does not seem so bad for an ELL. It is important to remember, however, that Josue is taking courses with below grade-level expectations. For some schools in California, sheltered courses do count toward the a–g requirements (a set of required courses encompassing history, social science, lab science, English, math, foreign languages, arts, and college prep) needed for admission to the university system. The sheltered courses, which integrate language with content, taken in combination, will hardly prepare Josue for the kind of future that he deserves. If Josue wishes to attend college, these courses will not prepare him for the rigor and demands that he will encounter.

The ELL debriefing encourages a data talk similar to the one that has been written in this section, using the reflective questions included in the following section. The following section will also describe how to use the ELL shadowing information to further determine and focus on ELL needs systemically.

ELL Shadowing Protocol Data Triangulation

Student observation data regarding academic speaking and listening on the ELL Shadowing Protocol form demonstrated that Josue had few opportunities for academic oral language development. Over the two hours that Josue was observed, he had only one opportunity for academic oral language development, which occurred in his first period Algebra I class. This opportunity for academic speaking was not structured, so Josue only briefly took advantage of it. From the classroom observation data and Josue's achievement results, it is no wonder that Josue has actually regressed in speaking on the CELDT, the language proficiency assessment, since he had almost no opportunities to speak in the two classrooms in which he was observed. In fact, Josue has regressed in speaking levels over the past three years by moving back from a Level 4 for two years, to a Level 3 in his most recent assessment results for speaking. From these results, the educator might determine that more structured opportunities for classroom talk should be provided. Through a similar analysis, if this were true for most ELLs observed during the shadowing experience, then district or school efforts should be made toward training teachers to systemically embed academic oral language development into classrooms. An example of this can be found in Chapter 8 of the book.

The observation also demonstrated that although Josue tried intently to listen while in his Biology II class, he often did not know what he was listening for, as he was not required or expected to listen specifically in the lesson design. Again, although Josue caused no behavioral issues in the classroom setting, he needed to know which portions of the lecture and video shown were important and which were not. In this way, he would have benefited from a graphic organizer that caused him to listen for key vocabulary or specific information. Additionally, if Josue struggled with listening in this way, then many more students could have as well. Training teachers around the different ways to structure listening for ELLs, as well as practical strategies for doing this, would prove helpful to many students to be actively engaged.

The poster shown in Figure 6.12 includes key questions that schools may consider as they review the data collected from the ELL Shadowing experience. Once teachers have reflected on the trends and patterns from the ELL shadowing data, they can determine next steps that have been triangulated from both the achievement data and the classroom observations. This creates buy-in when new strategies or teaching methods are introduced, so it no longer is a top-down approach to change.

TARGETING PROFESSIONAL DEVELOPMENT ACCORDING TO ELL NEEDS

As participants in groups analyze data, as described previously, they will begin to see trends and themes regarding student needs. If the majority of ELLs at a particular school site have the same need in terms of academic oral language development, then professional development should be targeted in that vein. As the ELL shadowing data collected is used in conjunction with student assessment data, the specific needs of this student group can be targeted. Since staff development data also tells us that teachers need at least fifty hours of professional development in a particular focus area to create change, it is important to follow up shadowing by providing targeted professional development that will meet the needs of ELLs at each particular site. For example, if in the analysis it was found that most ELLs at a site were at the midrange of English language proficiency, with few systemic opportunities for academic oral language development, then

Figure 6.12 ELL Shadowing Data Reflection

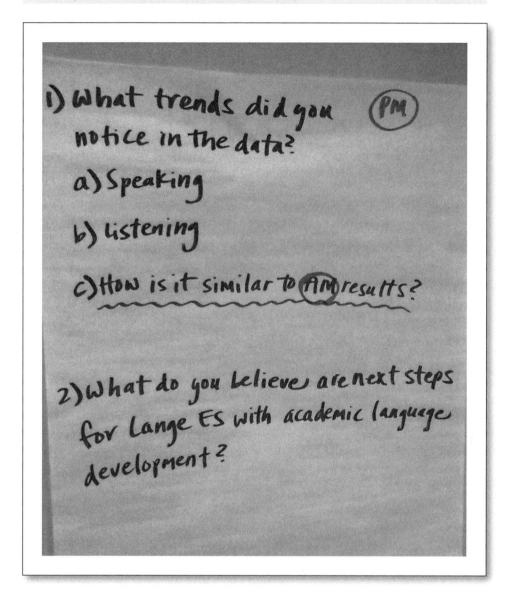

teachers might want to begin to incorporate academic language stems, along with a content area vocabulary word wall, in order to meet those language demands. ELLs at more midlevel and advanced levels of English language proficiency, with few opportunities for academic oral language development, might be ready for structured group work such as reciprocal teaching (more suggestions on next steps for professional development are presented in Chapter 10). In other words, the needs that emerge from the initial student assessment data, along with the aggregate trends of ELLs from the protocol site, should help direct and inform the professional development. The days of random, drive-by professional development are over in this time of intense student need and accountability. Such levels of data analysis, triangulated with classroom observation data from shadowing, should both create the level of urgency needed and create next steps. More information regarding follow-up trainings to shadowing will be addressed in subsequent chapters.

School Site ELL Shadowing

When planning a school site ELL shadowing training, it is important to train all teachers with the Day 1 content, in order to ensure that everyone is on the same page and has the same lens to observe students. At the school site, however, it is additionally important to make certain that a culture of trust and openness has already been set. If teachers are not used to being observed or having additional people in their classrooms, then ELL shadowing at one's own school site might not be the best option. If shadowing is completed at one's own site, the participant must be reminded that the shadowing training is about the experience of an ELL and not the teacher. Even so, teachers need to know that they will be in each other's classrooms, which often takes a level of trust for systems so that some of the results during the debriefing do not cause unnecessary alarm.

Once trust has been established at the school site level, it is important for organizers to conduct the same level of data analysis as suggested before—historical data on language proficiency assessments, state tests, as well as grades—for the level of ELL the system has determined that it would like to study. At the school site level, Day 1 of ELL shadowing can be conducted during district allotted professional development days. Remember that it is not advisable to conduct an ELL shadowing training without first training teachers on the importance of academic speaking and active listening on Day 1. Once this is done, substitute teachers can be used to cover those teachers who are in classrooms shadowing on Day 2. Depending on the size of the faculty, substitutes can be obtained for half of the staff members in the morning, and then the other half of the staff members can shadow in the afternoon. In this scenario, it is important that all teachers receive the same full-day training on listening and speaking, as well as how to shadow, before going into classrooms to shadow on Day 2. Using this model, the members of one group (often half of the school site staff) can shadow for two hours and then spend one hour debriefing what they saw, as well as looking for themes and patterns in the observation, alongside of the achievement data. The second group (the other half of the staff) can then do the same for the afternoon session. A more extensive debriefing, with data across both halves of the staff, can ensue when the staff members come together for their next faculty meeting. Figure 6.13 represents a schedule for ELL shadowing that can be used at a school site.

The schedule (Figure 6.13) can be modified for a full-day or half-day training session, depending on the amount of time available at the site. It is best to have a full day of training on Day 1, if at all possible, as many of the instructional strategies can be modeled and experienced only on the first day of the training. It is also important for all participants to become

Figure 6.13 Shadowing School Site Schedule

School Site ELL Shadowing Model	
Day 1 **Full- or Half-Day Professional Development**	**Day 2** **Half-Day Observations With Subs**

AM—Welcome and Agenda Review
 	
• Oral/Academic Language Development Overview
• Break
• Listening Overview
 	
PM—Shadowing Introduction
 	
• Practice With the Protocol
• Day 2 Agenda Overview/Logistics/ Student Profiles
• Closing and Evaluations
	AM—Brief Review of Protocol and ELL Profile (10–15 minutes)
	
	   o ELL Shadowing in Classrooms (2 hours)
	   o Debrief (45 minutes to 1 hour)
	
	Repeat same schedule in PM with the rest of faculty

grounded in the ELL shadowing process so that they are comfortable using the protocol and coding student interactions on Day 2. Figure 6.14 is an agenda for Day 2 of an ELL shadowing training at Dorothea Lange Elementary School in the Lucia Mar Unified School District in Arroyo Grande, California. At this school site, half of the faculty shadowed in the morning and the second half shadowed in the afternoon, with a whole school debriefing at the end of the second day.

Figure 6.14 ELL Shadowing School Site Schedule for Lange Elementary School

---

Lucia Mar Unified School District

Lange Elementary School

ELL Shadowing Agenda for May 9th

Group 1

8:30–8:55   ELL Shadowing Premeeting

    • Distribute Student Profiles

    • Reminders and Protocol Review

9:00–11:00   ELL Shadowing Observation in Classrooms

11:00–11:30 ELL Shadowing Mini Debriefing

Group 2

12:30–12:55	ELL Shadowing Premeeting
	• Distribute Student Profiles
	• Reminders and Protocol Review
1:00–3:00	ELL Shadowing Observation in Classrooms
3:00–3:30	ELL Shadowing Mini Debriefing
3:30-4:00	Whole School Trends and Debriefing Patterns

Additional ELL shadowing schedules will be presented in Chapter 10. The following chapter will demonstrate how to utilize specific components of the ELL Shadowing Protocol.

REFERENCES

Carstens, L. (2003a). *Do's and don'ts of shadowing.* PowerPoint presentation at ELL shadowing training for LAUSD, Local District 6, Commerce, CA.

Gibbons, P. (2002). *Scaffolding language, scaffolding learning: Teaching second language learners in the mainstream classroom.* Portsmouth, NH: Heinemann.

Olsen, L. (2010). *Reparable harm: Fulfilling the unkept promise of educational opportunity for California's long-term English learners.* Long Beach, CA: Californians Together. Available at http://www.californianstogether.org/

7

How to Use the Shadowing Protocol

So far, we have learned how to use the English Language Learner (ELL) shadowing protocol in order to collect data on academic speaking and listening. This chapter will focus in on how to utilize all of the other components of the ELL shadowing protocol for classroom data collection. As a review, in using the ELL shadowing protocol, teachers should only monitor, at the top of every five-minute interval, who the primary speaker is—either the student or teacher—as well as who the primary speaker is speaking to (see Chapter 4 for more on this). Educators should also remember that only *academic speaking* (not social talk) is to be noted and that only what is happening *most* at the beginning of the five-minute interval should be listed. Any additional information can be listed under the comments section. Also, the types of listening involved in the interaction are also monitored on the protocol, whether it is one way or two way. One-way listening is an interaction where students take in information, such as a lecture. Two-way listening is when your ELL asks for clarification or engages in a dialogue. Figure 7.1 represents the four categories for listening that will be monitored using the ELL shadowing protocol.

Typically, in one-way listening, there is no room for clarification or questions. In contrast, two-way listening allows for clarification to be made, because the interaction is dialogue based. That is, the interaction is considered a conversation (see more about this in Chapter 5). Throughout

Figure 7.1 Four Categories for Listening on Protocol

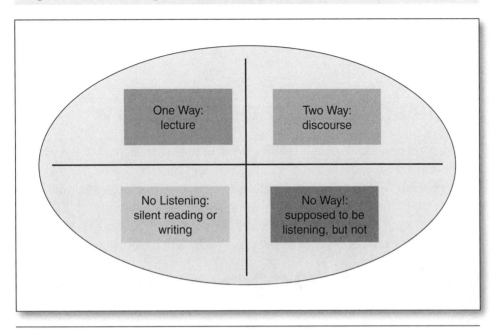

Source: Adapted from Gibbons (2002).

the ELL shadowing project, participants are often astounded by the fact that the teacher will do most of the talking, with much of the interaction being lecture based, despite the fact that the ELLs need many opportunities to practice language in order to develop it. Figure 7.2 visually represents different examples and contexts in which students can listen.

Figure 7.2 Listening Contexts

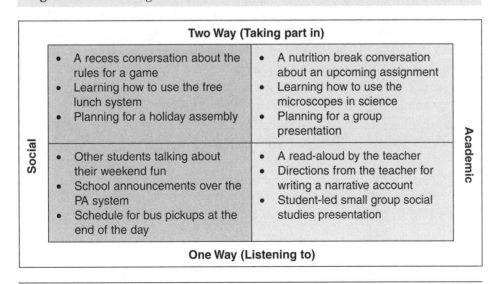

Source: Adapted from Gibbons (2002).

It is important for educators to understand the listening contexts, as they will be monitoring them on the ELL shadowing protocol. Generally, participants need to understand that one-way listening is lecture based and two-way listening is dialogue based (for more on this see Chapter 5, The Importance of Active Listening).

ELL SHADOWING PROTOCOL OVERVIEW

This section will explain step-by-step how to use each section of the protocol. Before actually shadowing an ELL, participants should be taught how to thoroughly use the protocol before they ever enter a classroom. This ensures that all educators have the same lens when they enter classrooms and are looking for the same evidence. Figure 7.3 is a blank ELL shadowing protocol. Each section of the protocol form will be explained in subsequent sections.

From Figure 7.3, it is evident that there are seven sections to the ELL shadowing protocol:

1. ELL student's demographic information (top portion of the protocol)

2. Time interval (noted at every five minutes)

3. Specific student activity to be taken down at the top of every five-minute interval

4. Academic speaking codes/interactions

5. Academic listening codes/interactions

6. Coding for students who are not listening or required to listen

7. Comments section

Each of these sections will be explained thoroughly in the segments to follow.

ELL Demographic Information

The top portion, or the demographic information of the ELL shadowing protocol, should be filled out on the morning of Day 2 of the ELL shadowing training. This is when participants receive their ELL shadowing profile information. Schools or districts may also choose to pass out the ELL Profile Forms to participants at the end of Day 1 of the ELL shadowing training. If this is the case, then it is important to remind participants to bring their profile forms with them on Day 2 of the training. The demographic information on the protocol form includes the language proficiency level (ELD level in California schools), gender, and grade level, as well as years in U.S. schools and in the district. This information is important so that the participants know who they are shadowing so that they can properly analyze student data once they

Figure 7.3   Blank ELL Shadowing Protocol

Student: _____   School: _____   ELD Level: _____

Gender: _____   Grade Level: _____   Years in US Schools: _____   Years in District: _____

Time	Specific Student Activity/Location of Student Five-Minute Intervals	Academic Speaking (check one)	Academic Listening One Way or Two Way (check one)	Student Is Not Listening (check one)	Comments
		☐ Student to student—*1* ☐ Student to teacher—*2* ☐ Student to small group—*3* ☐ Student to whole class—*4* ☐ Teacher to student—*5* ☐ Teacher to small group—*6* ☐ Teacher to whole class—*7*	**One way or two way** ☐ Student listening mostly to student—*1* ☐ Student listening mostly to teacher—*2* ☐ Student listening mostly to small group—*3* ☐ Student listening mostly to whole class—*4*	☐ Reading or writing silently—*1* ☐ Student is off-task—*2*	
		☐ Student to student—*1* ☐ Student to teacher—*2* ☐ Student to small group—*3* ☐ Student to whole class—*4* ☐ Teacher to student—*5* ☐ Teacher to small group—*6* ☐ Teacher to whole class—*7*	**One way or two way** ☐ Student listening mostly to student—*1* ☐ Student listening mostly to teacher—*2* ☐ Student listening mostly to small group—*3* ☐ Student listening mostly to whole class—*4*	☐ Reading or writing silently—*1* ☐ Student is off-task—*2*	

have completed their observations. Figure 7.4 is the demographic section of the ELL Shadowing Form.

Figure 7.4 Demographic Information of ELL Shadowing Protocol

Student: _____	School: _____	ELD Level: _____
Gender: _____	Grade Level: _____ Years in US Schools: _____	Years in District: _____

ELLs who are shadowed should be selected according to the language proficiency level of the school site or district need, in order to analyze their academic speaking and listening experiences across an entire system. This information, then, also assists with next steps in determining and differentiating professional development at that specific level.

Tracking Time on ELL Shadowing Protocol

The first column on the ELL shadowing protocol requires participants to write down the exact time of each interaction at every five-minute interval (see Figure 7.5 highlighted).

Figure 7.5 ELL Shadowing Protocol Highlighted for Time

Time	Specific Student Activity/ Location of Student Five-Minute Intervals	Academic Speaking (check one)	Academic Listening One Way or Two Way (check one)	Student Is Not Listening (check one)	Comments
8:15		☐ Student to student—**1** ☐ Student to teacher—**2** ☐ Student to small group—**3** ☐ Student to whole class—**4** ☐ Teacher to student—**5** ☐ Teacher to small group—**6** ☐ Teacher to whole class—**7**	**One way or two way** ☐ Student listening mostly to student—**1** ☐ Student listening mostly to teacher—**2** ☐ Student listening mostly to small group—**3** ☐ Student listening mostly to whole class—**4**	☐ Reading or writing silently—**1** ☐ Student is off-task—**2**	

In the first column above, participants should note the exact time that they are recording their ELL's activities. This should then be done at every five-minute interval from the first interaction recorded. That is, if the observation begins at 8:15 a.m., then the second interaction should be written at 8:20 a.m. and so on. This ensures that there is a pattern and consistency in the way that student activities are recorded throughout the ELL shadowing observation. It is useful for the participants to have a watch or phone handy so that they can monitor time as accurately as possible. Classroom clocks are not always reliable or in working condition.

Tracking Student Activities on ELL Shadowing Protocol

The second column on the ELL shadowing protocol requires participants to note the exact activity and location of the student and what is taking place at every five-minute interval (see Figure 7.6 highlighted).

Figure 7.6 ELL Shadowing Protocol Highlighted for Student Activity

Time	Specific Student Activity/Location of Student Five-Minute Intervals	Academic Speaking (check one)	Academic Listening One Way or Two Way (check one)	Student Is Not Listening (check one)	Comment
	Josue completes his worksheet independently at his desk.	☐ Student to student—**1** ☐ Student to teacher—**2** ☐ Student to small group—**3** ☐ Student to whole class—**4** ☐ Teacher to student—**5** ☐ Teacher to small group—**6** ☐ Teacher to whole class—**7**	**One way or two way** ☐ Student listening mostly to student—**1** ☐ Student listening mostly to teacher—**2** ☐ Student listening mostly to small group—**3** ☐ Student listening mostly to whole class—**4**	☐ Reading or writing silently—**1** ☐ Student is off-task—**2**	

In the second column, it is important that participants take down what their ELLs are doing at the top of every five-minute interval only. That is, everything that is occurring during the entire five-minute interval should not be taken down, as in a running record. Instead, for interrater reliability reasons, whatever activity the ELL is participating in *first* and *most* at the start of the five-minute interval should be taken down. Any additional information regarding the five-minute time period is then recorded in the last column called the comments section (more about this section in the paragraphs to come).

Tracking Academic Speaking on ELL Shadowing Protocol

The third column on the ELL shadowing protocol requires participants to take down who is doing the academic speaking—the ELL or the teacher—at the top of the five-minute interval (see section highlighted in Figure 7.7).

Figure 7.7 ELL Shadowing Protocol Highlighted for Academic Speaking

Time	Specific Student Activity/Location of Student Five-Minute Intervals	Academic Speaking (check one)	Academic Listening One Way or Two Way (check one)	Student Is Not Listening (check one)	Comments
		☐ Student to student—*1* ☐ Student to teacher—*2* ☐ Student to small group—*3* ☐ Student to whole class—*4* ☐ Teacher to student—*5* ☐ Teacher to small group—*6* ☐ Teacher to whole class—*7*	**One way or two way** ☐ Student listening mostly to student—*1* ☐ Student listening mostly to teacher—*2* ☐ Student listening mostly to small group—*3* ☐ Student listening mostly to whole class—*4*	☐ Reading or writing silently—*1* ☐ Student is off-task—*2*	

In the third column, notice that there is a section to check off the primary person speaking at the top of the five-minute interval. Although the ELL shadowing observation is about the student, there is a section for teacher talk so that there is a way to take down data around who is talking *most* during the observation. In this way, note that by checking off boxes 1 through 4 participants are noting *student* talk. Similarly, by checking off boxes 5 through 7, *teacher* talk is noted during the interaction. The teacher talk coding system was added to the ELL shadowing form in order to be able to code the segments of time when students were not speaking, as teacher talk was the most frequent occurrence of speaking when students were not speaking. It is also important for participants to remember that only academic speaking experiences should be taken down. Social talk, such as friendly conversations or playground conversations, should not be coded as academic speaking. Instead, participants can make note of such interactions in the comments section of the observation form (to be discussed later). For more on the difference between academic and social speaking, see Chapter 4.

Tracking Academic Listening on ELL Shadowing Protocol

The fourth column on the ELL shadowing protocol, highlighted below, requires that participants record what kind of academic listening the student is experiencing—one way or two way at the top of the five-minute interval (see Figure 7.8 highlighted).

Figure 7.8   ELL Shadowing Protocol Highlighted for Academic Listening

Time	Specific Student Activity/Location of Student Five-Minute Intervals	Academic Speaking (check one)	Academic Listening One Way or Two Way (check one)	Student Is Not Listening (check one)	Comments
		☐ Student to student—*1* ☐ Student to teacher—*2* ☐ Student to small group—*3* ☐ Student to whole class—*4* ☐ Teacher to student—*5* ☐ Teacher to small group—*6* ☐ Teacher to whole class—*7*	**One way or two way** ☐ Student listening mostly to student—*1* ☐ Student listening mostly to teacher—*2* ☐ Student listening mostly to small group—*3* ☐ Student listening mostly to whole class—*4*	☐ Reading or writing silently—*1* ☐ Student is off-task—*2*	

In the fourth column, participants are asked to check off the kind of listening that the ELL is engaged in at the top of the five-minute interval. Notice that unlike the academic speaking column, participants are only checking off to whom the student is listening most. In this section, we are not recording what the teacher is doing at all. There are four coding options here:

1. Student listening mostly to a student (as in Think-Pair-Share)

2. Student listening mostly to a teacher (as in a lecture)

3. Student listening mostly to a small group (as in reciprocal teaching)

4. Student listening mostly to the whole class (as in choral reading or singing)

For more information on the contexts and kinds of listening (academic or social), see Chapter 5.

Tracking Students Not Listening or Not Required to Listen on the ELL Shadowing Protocol

The fifth column on the ELL shadowing protocol requires participants to take down occurrences when students are not listening or are not required to listen (see Figure 7.9 highlighted).

Figure 7.9 ELL Shadowing Protocol Highlighted for Students Not Listening or Not Required to Listen

Time	Specific Student Activity/Location of Student Five-Minute Intervals	Academic Speaking (check one)	Academic Listening One Way or Two Way (check one)	Student Is Not Listening (check one)	Comments
		☐ Student to student—*1* ☐ Student to teacher—*2* ☐ Student to small group—*3* ☐ Student to whole class—*4* ☐ Teacher to student—*5* ☐ Teacher to small group—*6* ☐ Teacher to whole class—*7*	**One way or two way** ☐ Student listening mostly to student—*1* ☐ Student listening mostly to teacher—*2* ☐ Student listening mostly to small group—*3* ☐ Student listening mostly to whole class—*4*	☐ Reading or writing silently—*1* ☐ Student is off-task—*2*	

In the fifth column, participants have two options that should only be checked off when appropriate. The first box can be checked off when students are not listening, but they *should* be. This includes off-task behavior of any kind. The second box can be checked off when ELLs *are not* specifically required to listen but are not off-task. Examples of this include when students are required to read or write silently. This option is made available so that independent work and off-task behavior can be appropriately coded.

Tracking Comments on the ELL Shadowing Protocol

The sixth column on the ELL shadowing protocol requires participants to record comments (see Figure 7.10 highlighted).

Figure 7.10 ELL Shadowing Protocol Highlighted for Comments

Time	Specific Student Activity/ Location of Student Five-Minute Intervals	Academic Speaking (check one)	Academic Listening One Way or Two Way (check one)	Comments
		☐ Student to student—*1* ☐ Student to teacher—*2* ☐ Student to small group—*3* ☐ Student to whole class—*4* ☐ Teacher to student—*5* ☐ Teacher to small group—*6* ☐ Teacher to whole class—*7*	**One way or two way** ☐ Student listening mostly to student—*1* ☐ Student listening mostly to teacher—*2* ☐ Student listening mostly to small group—*3* ☐ Student listening mostly to whole class—*4*	

In the sixth column, participants take down additional comments that will be helpful in analyzing interactions once the observation is completed. Additional comments may include explanations that further clarify the activity that the ELL participated in or information regarding interactions that are unclear to the observer. Additionally, participants can take down comments that explain what occurred during the rest of the five-minute interval, which may not have been noted in the first column regarding the primary activity. The information in the comments section will later be analyzed for themes and patterns and provides important reasons why the specific phenomenon or activity may be occurring in the classroom setting.

Completed ELL Shadowing Protocol

Figure 7.11 demonstrates how to complete the ELL shadowing protocol, using examples of the kinds of interactions that might occur in the classroom setting. Below is a protocol that has been coded for a quick write.

Figure 7.11 ELL Shadowing Protocol With Quick-Write Example

		Student: Josue	School: Si Se Puede High School	ELD Level: Level 4—Early Advanced	

		Gender: Male	Grade Level: 10	Years in US Schools: 11 years	Years in District: 11 years

Time	Specific Student Activity/ Location of Student Five-Minute Intervals	Academic Speaking (check one)	Academic Listening One Way or Two Way (check one)	Student Is Not Listening (check one)	Comments
8:00 am	*Student participates in quick write regarding prompt, "What impacted you most about yesterday's reading?"*	☐ Student to student—**1** ☐ Student to teacher—**2** ☐ Student to small group—**3** ☐ Student to whole class—**4** ☐ Teacher to student—**5** ☐ Teacher to small group—**6** ☐ Teacher to whole class—**7**	**One way or two way** ☐ Student listening mostly to student—**1** ☐ Student listening mostly to teacher—**2** ☐ Student listening mostly to small group—**3** ☐ Student listening mostly to whole class—**4**	☑ Reading or writing silently—**1** ☐ Student is off-task—**2**	*Josue starts on task with writing, but doesn't seem to write very much. It seems like he could use some help to stay on task.*

Notice in the first column that the exact time—8:00 a.m.—has been recorded. In the second column, the activity, a quick write, and the exact prompt, have been taken down. The quick-write example has been coded in the fifth column, which allows participants to track occurrences when ELLs are not required to listen or are not listening. In this case, Josue is asked to respond to a writing prompt regarding material presented the day before, which does not require him to listen. Notice that in the final column, additional details about his actions—that Josue starts off strong, tapers off, and could use some help—have been recorded. The comments section is the place where any anecdotal information should be noted. It is important to take down the comments section information carefully, as it will often explain *why* the ELL is not engaging or interacting as we would like. As we analyze themes and trends from the comments section in the debriefing section, we can often determine additional instructional needs that the ELLs shadowed might have. The next few sets of examples will explain how several additional classroom situations should be coded.

Coding for Think-Pair-Share

Figure 7.12 demonstrates how a Think-Pair-Share exchange should be coded.

Figure 7.12 ELL Shadowing Protocol With Think-Pair-Share

Student: Josue		**School: Si Se Puede High School**		**LD Level: Level 4—Early Advanced**	
Gender: Male	**Grade Level: 10**	**Years in US Schools: 11 years**		**Years in District: 11 years**	
Time	**Specific Student Activity/ Location of Student Five-Minute Intervals**	**Academic Speaking (check one)**	**Academic Listening One Way or Two Way (check one)**	**Student Is Not Listening (check one)**	**Comments**
8:05 am	*Josue shares his quick-write prompt with his partner via Think-Pair-Share.*	☑ Student to student—*1* ☐ Student to teacher—*2* ☐ Student to small group—*3* ☐ Student to whole class—*4* ☐ Teacher to student—*5* ☐ Teacher to small group—*6* ☐ Teacher to whole class—*7*	**One way or two way** ☐ Student listening mostly to student—*1* ☐ Student listening mostly to teacher—*2* ☐ Student listening mostly to small group—*3* ☐ Student listening mostly to whole class—*4*	☐ Reading or writing silently—*1* ☐ Student is off-task—*2*	*Josue shares well and seems to stay on task with his conversation due to the sentence starter provided by the teacher.*

In the first column, note the next five-minute interval from the quick write—8:05 a.m.—has been taken down. Additionally, in the second column, the primary activity of Think-Pair-Share has been documented. Josue is now being asked to discuss his quick-write prompt, or what he learned from yesterday's class session, with the partner sitting next to him. Because he is talking to another student, this has been coded a 1 (student to student) for academic speaking. The comments section indicates that he is able to stay on task because of the sentence starter provided to him by the teacher. This is helpful information for teachers, as it demonstrates a scaffolding strategy that is helpful to Josue and perhaps other ELLs.

Coding for Teacher Lecture

Figure 7.13 demonstrates how a teacher lecture, or a time when the teacher is doing most of the talking, should be coded. Note that this has been coded for a fifteen-minute time segment.

At 8:10 a.m., the teacher gives general directions to the whole class regarding how they will use the class reading from the past few days in order to complete a group activity. The third column has been coded a 7 because the teacher is talking to the whole class. Additionally, the fourth column has been coded a 2 because Josue is listening to the teacher, as the comments also suggest. He is briefly heard telling his neighbor in Spanish that he wants to be the connector, which has been taken down in the comments section. He seems to be excited about working on a group activity.

At 8:15 a.m., the teacher begins to explain the specifics of how reciprocal teaching works, including each of the four distinctive roles: summarizer, questioner, predictor, and connector. The teacher explains how each role should be completed and passes out the graphic organizer for students to see. Since the teacher is doing most of the talking here, the third column is coded a 7. In the comments section, it has been noted that perhaps the teacher could have had all students, including Josue, take notes on the graphic organizer regarding each of the roles.

At 8:20 a.m., the teacher assigns an individual role to each student. Josue seems to be listening intently again for his role to be called out, so the fourth column is coded a 2 (listening mostly to the teacher). Since the teacher is still talking, the third column has been coded a 7 (teacher talking to whole class). Notice that additional comments have been recorded in the final column, including how Josue cheers when he finds out that he has been assigned the connector role.

Figure 7.13   ELL Shadowing Protocol With Teacher Lecture

Student: <u>Josue</u>   School: <u>Si Se Puede High School</u>   ELD Level: <u>Level 4—Early Advanced</u>

Gender: <u>Male</u>   Grade Level: <u>10</u>   Years in US Schools: <u>11 years</u>   Years in District: <u>11 years</u>

Time	Specific Student Activity/Location of Student Five-Minute Intervals	Academic Speaking (check one)	Academic Listening One Way or Two Way (check one)	Comments
8:10 am	*The teacher gives general directions for the next group activity, which will be reciprocal teaching, based on the reading completed the day before.*	☐ Student to student—*1* ☐ Student to teacher—*2* ☐ Student to small group—*3* ☐ Student to whole class—*4* ☐ Teacher to student—*5* ☐ Teacher to small group—*6* ☑ Teacher to whole class—*7*	**One way or two way** ☐ Student listening mostly to student—*1* ☑ Student listening mostly to teacher—*2* ☐ Student listening mostly to small group—*3* ☐ Student listening mostly to whole class—*4*	*The teacher explains how students will use the reading from the previous day's class session to complete a group activity called reciprocal teaching. Josue seems to be excited about working in a group and listens for his role. In Spanish, he tells his friend that he wants to be the connector.*
8:15 am	*The teacher explains each role associated with reciprocal teaching and how to complete it.*	☐ Student to student—*1* ☐ Student to teacher—*2* ☐ Student to small group—*3* ☐ Student to whole class—*4* ☐ Teacher to student—*5* ☐ Teacher to small group—*6* ☑ Teacher to whole class—*7*	**One way or two way** ☐ Student listening mostly to student—*1* ☑ Student listening mostly to teacher—*2* ☐ Student listening mostly to small group—*3* ☐ Student listening mostly to whole class—*4*	*Josue seems to be a bit off-task during this segment of the directions. He could use some structure for listening here. Maybe require notes on graphic organizer?*
8:20 am	*The teacher assigns specific roles associated with reciprocal teaching to each student.*	☐ Student to student—*1* ☐ Student to teacher—*2* ☐ Student to small group—*3* ☐ Student to whole class—*4* ☐ Teacher to student—*5* ☐ Teacher to small group—*6* ☑ Teacher to whole class—*7*	**One way or two way** ☐ Student listening mostly to student—*1* ☑ Student listening mostly to teacher—*2* ☐ Student listening mostly to small group—*3* ☐ Student listening mostly to whole class—*4*	*Josue seems to be listening intently again for what his role will be. He is happy to find out that he will be the connector.*

Coding for Group Work

Figure 7.14 demonstrates how group work, like reciprocal teaching, should be coded. Notice again that this has been coded for a fifteen-minute segment.

At 8:25 a.m., Josue listens to his group members as they review the role that each person will be completing. Note that since Josue and the teacher are not the ones speaking, the third column has been left blank. Since Josue is listening, however, the fourth column has been coded a 3, as he listens to his group members intently. The comments section describes the interaction further.

At 8:30 a.m., Josue independently works on his reciprocal teaching role of connector, which has been coded a 2 (student reads or write silently) in the fifth column. Notice that the comments section describes him as conscientiously taking out his materials and working through the entire five-minute interval. At 8:35 a.m., Josue gets his first opportunity to talk to his small group regarding his group role. This exchange has been coded a 3 (student talking to a small group) in the third column. The comments section suggests that Josue has a caring and supportive group and that it encourages him when needed.

Continued Coding

During an ELL shadowing, educators would continue to code interactions this way at every five-minute interval, for two hours or up to four hours. As demonstrated in the previous five-minute intervals, the shadowing project allows educators to begin to find patterns regarding who is doing most of the speaking in classrooms and what kinds of listening ELLs are often asked to undertake. Educators soon begin to notice that the primary speaker in classrooms is often the teacher, which was true for Josue in the previous example. In fact, in this example, Josue only received one opportunity to speak. Similarly, educators find that the listening interactions are often one way, or in lecture mode, with little room for questions or clarification on the part of the ELL. Again, this was Josue's experience in the examples noted throughout this chapter.

In the shadowing debriefing process, analyzing these student interactions across participants becomes essential in changing instructional practices systemically (see Chapter 8). Similarly, the shadowing project illuminates for teachers how the absence of opportunities for academic oral language development impacts ELL achievement. Through this process, educators are able to reflect on their own instructional practices, as well as how such practices may positively or negatively impact student achievement. For example, one teacher in the Los Angeles Unified School District's (LAUSD) District 6 stated, "The person talking most is the person who is learning most . . . and I'm doing most of the talking in my class!" This process, then, creates the urgency for changing instructional practice systematically across levels. In this way, teachers begin to see *why* they need to change their instructional practices in order to make more room for academic oral language development in the classroom setting. From the ELL shadowing experience, it is often teachers who want to take the lead around eliciting more talk

Figure 7.14 ELL Shadowing Protocol With Group Work

Student: Josue		School: Si Se Puede High School		ELD Level: Level 4—Early Advanced

Gender: Male	Grade Level: 10	Years in US Schools: 11 years	Years in District: 11 years

Time	Specific Student Activity/Location of Student Five-Minute Intervals	Academic Speaking (check one)	Academic Listening One Way or Two Way (check one)	Comments
8:25 am	Josue listens as his team members review each of their roles.	☐ Student to student—1 ☐ Student to teacher—2 ☐ Student to small group—3 ☐ Student to whole class—4 ☐ Teacher to student—5 ☐ Teacher to small group—6 ☐ Teacher to whole class—7	**One way or two way** ☐ Student listening mostly to student—1 ☐ Student listening mostly to teacher—2 ☑ Student listening mostly to small group—3 ☐ Student listening mostly to whole class—4	Josue moves his desk so that he is situated with his group members. He listens intently to his group members' plans.
8:30 am	Josue independently completes his connector role.	☐ Student to student—1 ☐ Student to teacher—2 ☐ Student to small group—3 ☐ Student to whole class—4 ☐ Teacher to student—5 ☐ Teacher to small group—6 ☐ Teacher to whole class—7	**One way or two way** ☐ Student listening mostly to student—1 ☐ Student listening mostly to teacher—2 ☐ Student listening mostly to small group—3 ☐ Student listening mostly to whole class—4	Josue takes out his reading materials from the day before. He works well the entire five-minute interval.
8:35 am	Josue begins to share his connector role with the rest of his group.	☐ Student to student—1 ☐ Student to teacher—2 ☑ Student to small group—3 ☐ Student to whole class—4 ☐ Teacher to student—5 ☐ Teacher to small group—6 ☐ Teacher to whole class—7	**One way or two way** ☐ Student listening mostly to student—1 ☐ Student listening mostly to teacher—2 ☐ Student listening mostly to small group—3 ☐ Student listening mostly to whole class—4	Josue gets to speak! He seems to be interested because he got the group role he wanted. The rest of his group tries to support him.

across a school day. From this experience, the results and next steps should immediately be analyzed and leveraged in order to bring about change for ELLs.

REFERENCES

Carstens, L. (2003b, March 3). *Four quadrants of listening.* PowerPoint presentation at ELL shadowing training for LAUSD, Local District 6, Commerce, CA.

Carstens, L. (2003c, March 3). *Modified Nunan listening examples.* PowerPoint presentation at ELL shadowing training for LAUSD, Local District 6, Commerce, CA.

SECTION IV

Debriefing the Shadowing Experience

8

Analyzing and Reflecting on the Results of Shadowing

DEBRIEFING THE ELL SHADOWING EXPERIENCE

Once the data on academic speaking and listening have been captured individually, an aggregate of the English Language Learner (ELL) shadowing experience is taken, either by level (elementary, middle, or high school), school site (if shadowing occurred at multiple school sites), or both by tallying responses by mode for academic speaking and listening. The aggregate then identifies the need that students have regarding the role of academic speaking and listening, at each site or level. Additionally, the aggregate should identify professional development needs at each site level. The power of ELL shadowing comes both from the classroom observation itself and from the follow-up discussions and plans that occur as a result of the experience. It is important to remember that ELL shadowing is not a panacea. It is a way to create change across a system when specific planning and follow-up is completed after the ELL shadowing experience. The aggregate numbers from shadowing allow participants to quantify what they just saw happening with their own ELL. That is, many ELLs often experience the fate of spending less than 2 percent of their school day in academic oral language development. When this phenomenon is experienced both by the individual and by groups of educators, the urgency around the systemic need and change required becomes palpable. Groups of educators almost never want to turn away without doing something to effect change.

There are four steps to the ELL shadowing debriefing session on Day 2 of the training:

1. ELL shadowing reflection process

2. Tallying of academic speaking and listening

3. Two-word response analysis

4. ELL data talk triangulation of data

The following section will explain each of those processes.

ELL Shadowing Reflection

The ELL shadowing debriefing session begins with the ELL Shadowing Experience: Reflection form, part of which is shown in Figure 8.1 (for the full form, see Appendix A, page 124, or http://www.corwin.com/ellshadowing). This reflection process includes a series of questions that allow the participants to think about what they just experienced when shadowing their ELLs. These questions also allow participants to go back to the Gibbons materials from Day 1 of the training and to reflect on some of the changes that they might want to adopt systematically at their own sites. The ELL shadowing reflection questions begin individually and then move out toward finding themes and patterns across participants. Notice each of the questions in Figure 8.1, which are explained in detail in subsequent paragraphs.

Figure 8.1 ELL Shadowing Experience: Reflection

1. Write a short reflection on your observation of the student's learning experience.

2. Share your written experience with a partner. Identify common elements.

3. As a group of three or more, identify common elements. Select someone at your table to share common elements with the entire group.

4. Review "Looking at Classroom Talk" in Gibbons (2002), pp. 17–18. Think about your student. Think about _____ (name of student). Did you observe your student in any group work?

5. If the eight characteristics were in place within each classroom, would the observation expereience have been the same?

Figure 8.1 demonstrates the first set of questions that participants will use to debrief the ELL shadowing experience. The five questions are important for the following reasons:

1. **Write a short reflection on your observation of the student's learning experience.** This question is completed individually by each participant. Participants should be instructed to write down key impressions regarding what they just experienced with ELL shadowing. I often ask participants to think about what the ELL himself or herself might say about what school was like as participants observed. If participants choose this route for their reflection, they do not have to write with an ELL's voice or in the first person. This is just a way for participants, if they are struggling with how to do it, to describe their ELL's experience in school. These reflections can come from either the quantitative (coding) or the qualitative (comments) sections of the ELL shadowing observation form.

2. **Share your written experience with a partner. Identify common elements.** Participants turn and talk to a partner regarding what they experienced with their own ELL. Commonalities, themes, and patterns, between both participants, should be taken down for this question. If there are only differences between the two experiences, partners should record them and note them as such.

3. **As a group of three or more, identify common elements. Select someone at your table to share common elements with the entire group.** This question can be completed by three participants at a table or with the entire group. Participants can summarize commonalities at each table and then have one person share them with the entire group. This allows participants to further see that across grades or levels, there are patterns of needs that should be addressed.

4. **Review "Looking at Classroom Talk" (Gibbons (2002), pp. 17–18). Think about your student. Think about _____ (name of student). Did you observe your student in any group work?** This question allows participants to go back into Gibbons's work from Day 1 of the training and think through the benefits of student talk for ELLs. Participants can note exactly what kind of group work students were engaged in, if the participants saw it taking place. If no group work was observed, participants can reflect on how their ELLs *would have* benefited, had group work been available.

5. **If the eight characteristics (see Figure 8.2) were in place within each classroom, would the observation experience have been the same?** The final question connects participants with the Eight Characteristics of Productive Group Work from Gibbons's work (which is shown in Figure 8.2), presented on Day 1 of the training.

Figure 8.2   Eight Characteristics of Productive Group Work for ELL Students

1. Clear and explicit instructions are provided.	5. The task is integrated with a broader topic.
2. Talk is necessary for the task.	6. All children are involved.
3. There is a clear outcome.	7. Students have enough time.
4. The task is cognitively appropriate.	8. Students know how to work in groups.

Source: Adapted from Gibbons (2002), pp. 20–28.

Participants should document any of the eight characteristics of productive group work introduced on Day 1 of the training, if they were observed in the classroom setting. If these characteristics were not observed, participants should note how the ELL's experience *could have* been enhanced as a result of the characteristics. It is important to remember that part of the answer to the lack of oral academic language experiences encountered by ELLs comes from ensuring that group work is used to elicit more language and group work is structured so it can be productive and effective.

Two-Word Response Summary

Once the ELL shadowing experience reflection form has been completed and reviewed by the group, participants should be asked to synthesize their ELL's overall experience using two adjectives that can be written at the top of their reflection form. Participants are then asked to share one word with the entire group, while someone writes them on poster paper or on a whiteboard. Any words that are duplicated should be tallied. For example, during ELL shadowing trainings, I often hear the words *invisible* and *silent* used to describe what was experienced regarding an ELL's day in school. For the participants, the process of hearing these words out loud further makes concrete that the needs of ELLs are vast and that we all must do something about them. Figure 8.3 provides the step-by-step directions for the two-word response process.

The power of seeing, in two descriptive words, that the needs of ELLs were so similar and common further solidifies for the group the consciousness around the next steps that must be taken in order to change instruction systemically. Organizers of the training may also ask participants to write their words on sticky notes, which can then be sorted into commonalities. It is still encouraged that participants read their words out loud, before placing them on posters so that everyone hears the power of the words that have described the ELL's experience. Commonalities can then be shared with the organizers of the training, in order to emphasize the patterns and themes emerging.

Figure 8.3 Two-Word Shadowing Synthesis

- Select two words to describe your ELL's experience in school today.
- Share your two words with your group and tally any words that were found in common.
- As an entire group, share the commonalities that were found within each small group.

ELL Data Talk

After the two-word ELL shadowing synthesis is completed, the ELL data talk should be used. This process allows participants to triangulate the achievement data provided for their ELL student with the classroom observations collected. Since participants have already reviewed their ELL's achievement data before they observed the student, they should now look for possible reasons for the achievement progress—or lack of progress—from what they saw in the classroom. For example, if it was discovered that the ELL had very few academic oral language development opportunities, then participants can begin to discuss how structuring Think-Pair-Share or having more productive group work opportunities would elicit more academic oral language in the classroom setting. Figure 8.4 outlines the way that the ELL data talk session should be structured using the Think-Pair-Share structure.

Figure 8.4 ELL Data Talk

Tell Your Partner About Your ELL

- Language Proficiency Assessment scores (overall and by domain)
- State Achievement Scores scores (ELA and Math)
- Years in country/school
  - Is the student progressing one level per year on the CELDT from when he or she arrived?

What additional information did the shadowing observation give you about your student?

Participants should be instructed to turn to a table partner and interview him or her regarding the ELL shadowed. They should pay careful attention to the following details:

- English language proficiency scores: The state English language proficiency scores should be analyzed, both year by year for the past three years and for each literacy domain (in California, these scores are given for listening, speaking, reading, and writing, as well as an overall score). Participants should pay careful attention to see if their ELL has progressed one level per year in each of the domains of language. These scores can then be compared to the progress being made in grades in the ELL's English language development course, as well as the classroom observation of that course, if participants shadowed there.

- State assessment results: The state grade-level assessment should similarly be analyzed for year-to-year progress. It should be noted if ELLs are making progress each year or regressing in achievement. These scores can then be compared to the progress the ELL is making in his or her math and English courses, as well as the classroom observation of that course, if participants shadowed there.

- Years in country: Participants should carefully note the number of years their ELL has been in school, compared to the level of progress that the student has been making since first coming into the United States. Both second-language theorists and the U.S. Department of Education would like ELLs to progress one level per year.

- Additional information: Any additional information, including information recorded in the comments section, should be discussed here. For example, if the ELL seemed tired or off-task or on-task and resilient, that information should be noted here.

The achievement data information should then be triangulated with the classroom observation data collected. This process should provide reasons why certain achievement results might be occurring. For example, if your ELL has not been making progress in listening on the language proficiency assessment (in California, the California English Language Development Test, or CELDT), perhaps the student was also struggling to pay attention in the classes in which he was observed. Such information will assist with recommendations and next steps for the ELL in the future.

Tally Responses

The final step in the ELL shadowing debriefing session should be to tally the number of responses for the academic speaking, listening, no/not listening, and comments sections of the ELL shadowing protocol (see Figure 8.5). The following section describes what participants should do as they tally the responses that were taken down during the ELL shadowing observation.

Figure 8.5 Tallying Responses

- Count up each of the Academic Speaking and Academic Listening components.
  - Tally the results on the poster.
- Synthesize your comments onto two sticky notes.

Participants should go through each of their ELL shadowing forms and complete the following for each section:

1. **Academic speaking:** Participants should count the number of 1 (student to student), 2 (student to teacher), 3 (student to small group), 4 (student to whole class), 5 (teacher to student), 6 (teacher to small group), and 7 (teacher to whole class) boxes that were checked off.

2. **Academic listening:** Count the number of 1 (student to student), 2 (student to teacher), 3 (student to small group), and 4 (student to whole class) boxes that were checked off.

3. **Student not listening/no listening:** Count the number of 1 (reading or writing silently) and 2 (student not listening) boxes that were checked off.

4. **Comments:** Participants should summarize all of their comments from the comments section on two sticky notes.

The ELL Shadowing Protocol in Figure 8.6 demonstrates how items can be tallied for each section.

Figure 8.6 Tallying ELL Shadowing Marks

Academic Speaking (check one)	Academic Listening One Way or Two Way (check one)	Student Is Not Listening (check one)	Comments
❏ Student to student—1	❏ One way or two way	❏ Reading or writing silently—1	❏
❏ //////	❏ Student listening mostly to student—1	❏ //////////////	
❏ Student to teacher—2	❏ //////	❏ Student is off-task—2	

Academic Speaking (check one)	Academic Listening One Way or Two Way (check one)	Student Is Not Listening (check one)	Comments
❑ ////	❑ Student listening mostly to teacher—2	❑ //////////	
❑ Student to small group—3	❑ ///////////////		
❑ Student to whole class—4	❑ Student listening mostly to small group—3		
❑ Teacher to student—5	❑ Student listening mostly to whole class—4		
❑ Teacher to small group—6	❑		
❑ Teacher to whole class—7			
❑ /////////////////			

Figure 8.6 visually represents the sections of the ELL shadowing form that should be tallied by participants. Organizers of the training should create poster-sized versions of these four sections of the protocol, making them large enough so that participants can physically tally their responses using markers. Participants will then place their sticky note summaries in the last column, which should then be sorted by theme and patterns. Figure 8.7 is a picture of a completed ELL Shadowing Analysis Sheet for two-day ELL shadowing training.

Once the tallies have been counted for each section, the most common mode under each section should be circled and shared with the group for further triangulation, with both the research literature and the ELL shadowing observations in the room. This process further demonstrates to participants what may need to change instructionally for ELLs in order to change academic achievement systemically. The analysis also allows participants to see manifested in the room, with the tallies, that ELLs do indeed spend less than 2 percent of the average school day in academic speaking (August, 2003). The percentage is no longer esoteric in nature but becomes real and alive in the room. Physically seeing these tally marks quantifies the data and also allows participants to make decisions regarding what next steps should come after the ELL shadowing experience. The following chapter will describe how to systemically leverage change from ELL shadowing.

Figure 8.7 ELL Shadowing Data Analysis

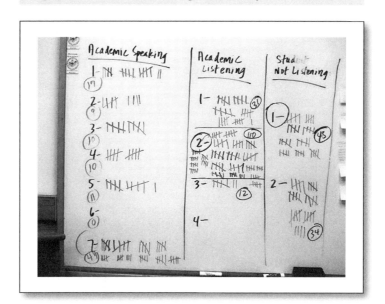

REFERENCES

August, D. (2003). PowerPoint presentation at the ELL Colloquium in Los Angeles Unified School District, Local District 6, Commerce, CA.

Gibbons, P. (2002). *Scaffolding language, scaffolding learning: Teaching second language learners in the mainstream classroom.* Portsmouth, NH: Heinemann.

9

Using the Results to Leverage Change

Once the data have been analyzed and trends determined, a useful tool for determining teacher-level need is the English Language Learner (ELL) Shadowing Next Steps: Needs Assessment form. Having been exposed to Think-Pair-Share, Teacher-Guided Reporting, and productive group work on Days 1 and 2 of the ELL shadowing training, it is important for participating educators to determine where they feel most comfortable entering into professional development using these academic oral language development strategies. These three strategies are also research-based ways to further engage all students and bring up the 2 percent of academic oral language development that ELLs typically engage in. Once academic oral language development has been amply developed, other components of academic language development—syntax, grammar, and vocabulary development—can also be incorporated into the classroom setting. This section will provide a process whereby the greatest areas of student need can be systemically focused on from the shadowing experience, with special attention to academic speaking and listening. It is important to remember, however, that because of the connections between speaking and writing, as well as listening and reading, educators are working on all aspects of academic language development when focusing on academic oral language development.

Figure 9.1 can be used to determine next steps and focus areas from the two-day ELL shadowing training. To begin, the first set of questions should be completed as a school team, and then the needs assessment (see Appendix A, page 123, or http://www.corwin.com/ellshadowing) should be completed individually. This process allows school teams to begin thinking collectively about how to systemically address the needs of ELLs.

Figure 9.1 School Reflection Questions

School Reflection

- What urgency did this shadowing experience illuminate for you?
- Where in the ALD spectrum might students at your grade level benefit most?
  - Think-Pair-Share
  - Teacher-Guided Reporting
  - Productive Group Work
- What planning/next steps are needed?

The questions in Figure 9.1 are asked for the following reasons:

1. **What urgency did this shadowing experience illuminate for you?** This open-ended question allows participants to begin to consider that the sense of urgency from what was experienced must now become a plan in order for change to come about.

2. **Where in the academic language development (ALD) spectrum might students at your grade level benefit most?** This question will be used in conjunction with the needs assessment form, which asks participants to rank their level of comfort with each of the following academic language development strategies below (discussed in the next section):
   - Think-Pair-Share
   - Teacher-Guided Reporting
   - Productive Group Work

3. **What planning/next steps are needed?** This question allows participants to realize that their next steps must be explicitly laid out in order for them to take effect. A calendar planning form, the ALD Lesson Plan, can be found in Appendix B, page 135, and at http://www.corwin.com/ellshadowing, for this purpose.

ELL SHADOWING NEXT STEPS: NEEDS ASSESSMENT

Using the ELL Shadowing Next Steps: Needs Assessment Form (see Appendix A, page 123, or http://www.corwin.com/ellshadowing), educators are asked to rate their level of classroom need on a scale of 1 through 5 (1 being lowest and 5 being highest). This information, along with the student-level assessment results, should guide professional development efforts. Participants should fill this out individually and share results by school team, department, or grade level to find the most common area of need and entry point. This form can also be used by grade or department level to set goals and determine common next steps with academic oral language development. As teachers select strategies in common, they can begin to support each other, both in lesson design and in making adjustments to the ways in which strategies are utilized. The ELL Shadowing Next Steps: Needs Assessment Form is explained next and can be found in Appendix A, page 123, or at http://www.corwin.com/ellshadowing.

Although the ELL shadowing results and assessment data analysis will allow needs to emerge very clearly, educators should be able to determine where their professional development efforts should begin. Otherwise, participants may feel overwhelmed by the level of need that has emerged from the ELL shadowing experience. Educators can begin by focusing on what they ranked as their highest level of need and when they feel comfortable there, begin to embed other oral academic language strategies listed to their practice. It is important to note that systems—a school, district, or county office—should provide support and training in how to implement each of these strategies as a follow-up to ELL shadowing (information on how to do this can be found in the chapter that follows). Organizers of the training should embed and model these practices—Think-Pair-Share, Teacher-Guided Reporting, and productive group work—into the initial ELL shadowing training itself. However, it is also essential to provide follow-up on how to implement each strategy in a classroom setting, once the needs and focus areas have been determined from the ELL shadowing and data analysis itself. This will be described further in Chapter 10.

District Shadowing Options

Once educational systems have had their first ELL shadowing experience, they can choose to continue to shadow to monitor ELL progress in a variety of ways. Each of these options will be explained further in the section to come, along with entry points that a variety of districts have taken with ELL shadowing. Figure 9.2 lists some options for future ELL shadowing.

Additional ELL shadowing experiences can include, but are not limited to, the following options:

1. **Follow ELLs after providing schoolwide or districtwide personal development:** Once teachers have received follow-up training (see Chapter 10) on eliciting more oral academic language in the classroom using Think-Pair-Share and Teacher-Guided Reporting, they can go into each other's classrooms looking for evidence of how ELLs in those classrooms are responding to and benefiting from the strategies. Additionally, teachers can examine ELL student work in order to determine next steps for instruction and strategy

Figure 9.2 Future Shadowing Experiences

Next Steps

- Future shadowing experiences:
    - Follow ELLs after providing schoolwide or districtwide personal development
    - Look for use of productive group work in classrooms
    - Follow ELLs at a variety of levels (elementary visit secondary and secondary visit elementary, or ELD levels)

---

usage with this group of students. I use the tuning protocol with several of the schools I work with to analyze student work samples from the implementation of academic oral language development strategies.

2. **Look for use of productive group work in classrooms:** Once teachers have been trained in how to implement reciprocal teaching (where students use the reading roles of summarizer, connector, questioner, and predictor to discuss a reading selection) or another group work strategy, they may choose go into each other's classrooms (by grade level or department) with the eight elements of productive group work (see Chapter 4) from Gibbons's (2002) work, to determine how those characteristics are assisting ELLs. Teachers can also plan next steps for instruction by determining which elements might need to be utilized more frequently.

3. **Follow ELLs at a variety of levels (elementary visit secondary and secondary visit elementary, or by English language development [ELD] levels):** To determine how ELLs are progressing across a system, districts may have elementary schools visit secondary schools, and vice versa, to begin articulation across levels. This can also be done within feeder patterns or ELD levels; that is, elementary schools that feed into middle and high schools can shadow each other. Additionally, teachers who teach beginning-level ELD students can shadow ELLs at the end of the ELD spectrum in order to see their progression and needs.

All of these ideas for additional ELL shadowing options can assist with ensuring that the urgency apparent throughout the two-day experience does not wane. In essence, ELL shadowing can be a way both to determine baseline needs and to monitor progress once specific ELL needs have been identified. As a seasoned teacher in Stanislaus County, California, has said, "I believe that ELL shadowing should be done each year so that we can monitor the progress of our ELLs and our programs" (personal communication, Soto-Hinman, 2006).

District and School Entry Points

The Norwalk–La Mirada Unified School District in Norwalk, California, a district of 21,500 students and 23 percent ELLs, conducted a districtwide ELL shadowing training, which first began with administrators in the fall of 2010. As described in Chapter 6, all administrators, including district office administrators, first attended half-day trainings on how to shadow an ELL. The actual ELL shadowing training at school sites followed this, with a debriefing session by elementary, middle, and high school participants, on three subsequent Fridays (Day 1 and 2 agendas can be found in Figures 9.3 and 9.4).

Figure 9.3   Day 1 Agenda of ELL Shadowing Training for Norwalk–La Mirada Unified

Norwalk–La Mirada Unified School District
ELL Shadowing
DAY 1 AGENDA

8:00—Registration and Continental Breakfast

8:30—Welcome and Agenda Review

8:40—Oral Language and Development Review

10:00—Break

10:30—Listening Overview

12:00—Lunch

12:45—Shadowing Introduction/Practice With the Protocol

2:30—Day 2 Agenda Overview/Logistics/Student Profiles

3:00—Closing

PLEASE DON'T FORGET TO WEAR YOUR
DISTRICT ID TO THE OBSERVATION SCHOOL ON DAY 2.

Once the districtwide administrator training took place, several schools—one per level—volunteered to be model implementation sites for ELL shadowing with the district. This meant that a core group of teacher-leaders at each site decided to shadow ELLs and also to participate in the academic language development follow-up sessions with me as the facilitator. This group of teachers decided to work on the needs of ELLs. The district office and school site administrative teams decided to start with a small group of teachers at each school, to create model classrooms and excitement around shadowing and meeting the needs of

Figure 9.4 Day 2 Agenda of ELL Shadowing Training for Norwalk–La Mirada Unified

Norwalk–La Mirada Unified School District
ELL Shadowing
DAY 2 AGENDA
School Site Visit Information

Johnston Elementary School (October 8, 2010)

Meeting Room: G-2

Premeeting Time: 7:45 a.m.

Los Alisos Middle School (October 22, 2010)

Meeting Room: 104

Premeeting Time: 7:30 a.m.

John Glenn High School (October 29, 2010)

Meeting Room: Library

Premeeting Time: 7:50 a.m.

8:00–10:00 a.m.—ELL Shadowing

10:00 a.m.—Break/Recess

10:15 a.m.—Shadowing Debriefing

11:15 a.m.—Wrap Up, Evaluations, PD Survey, Next Steps

ELLs. At the high school level, six teachers from across the content areas met on five different dates in the spring of 2011 to learn to shadow, debrief the experience, and begin to embed academic language development strategies systemically into their instruction with ELLs. This small group of willing teachers, whose work then caused additional excitement, provided a powerful way to replicate the administrator ELL shadowing experience. Also, once teachers began using the ALD strategies, additional teachers were encouraged to observe these best practices in action and to shadow an ELL themselves. This process, then, becomes a significant way to leverage change from the ELL shadowing experience. First, starting with a small group of teachers and then adding the rest of the staff, word soon spread about the power of the experience. This shows that it is important to remember that true systemic change often begins small. Teachers must feel that they have a voice in the change process and can choose entry points and strategies, especially at the beginning of the professional development sequence. The ELL Shadowing Next Steps: Needs Assessment can be used for that purpose and is included in Figure 9.5; in Appendix A, page 123; and at http://www.corwin.com/ellshadowing.

Figure 9.5 describes the ELL shadowing follow-up regarding academic language development, which should be used with all teachers and administrators once they have shadowed an ELL.

Figure 9.5 ELL Shadowing Next Steps: Needs Assessment

On a scale of 1 through 5, with 1 being lowest and 5 being highest, which of the following areas do you consider to be the greatest need in your classroom?

1. Think-Pair-Share

    1   2   3   4   5

Comments:

_____

_____

2. Teacher-Guided Reporting

Use of open-ended questions (requiring more than one-word responses)

    1   2   3   4   5

Asking for linguistic clarification (grammar, specific language, etc.)

    1   2   3   4   5

Encouragement

    1   2   3   4   5

Recasting (restating student responses in academic language)

    1   2   3   4   5

Comments:

_____

3. Productive Group Work (e.g., Reciprocal Teaching, Socratic Seminar, Literature Circles, etc.)

    1   2   3   4   5

Comments:

_____

REFERENCE

Gibbons, P. (2002). *Scaffolding language, scaffolding learning: Teaching second language learners in the mainstream classroom.* Portsmouth, NH: Heinemann.

SECTION V

Next Steps With ELL Shadowing

10

Next Steps and Follow-up to ELL Shadowing

ELL FOLLOW-UP ON ACADEMIC LANGUAGE DEVELOPMENT

English Language Learner (ELL) shadowing is the beginning of the learning and tailoring of needs for ELLs. ELL shadowing creates the awareness, but there must be a clear and focused plan to change practices for results to change for ELLs. Once next steps have been determined from the ELL shadowing experience, there must be ongoing professional development for teachers for ELLs to benefit from the changes in practices. This chapter will uncover three strategies that can be used to elicit more academic oral language development in the classroom setting.

Think-Pair-Share

Think-Pair-Share is one of the best ways to begin to embed more academic oral language development in a classroom setting. This oral language scaffold creates accountability for talk on the part of the student and is a good way for teachers to explore and begin to incorporate more academic oral language in a classroom setting. As mentioned in Chapter 4, August and Shanahan (2006) suggest that oral language development is the foundation of literacy. The academic oral language benefits for ELLs are expansive. Often, students are more comfortable presenting ideas to a group, especially when they have the support of a partner. Additionally, students' ideas, especially ELLs, become more refined through this three-step process. If, according to August and Shanahan (2006) on the National Literacy Panel report, ELLs also benefit from more time and practice with content, the Think-Pair-Share process allows those ideas to become developed over time. If ELLs are sharing with partners slightly above their level, the ELLs will benefit from hearing more language and higher levels of language, which they can then recycle in their own response. There should be times, however, when higher end students are grouped together so that they are also challenged.

If the benefits of academic oral language development structure are expansive, then as educators we must find ways and opportunities for students to talk in a linguistically rich environment. Pressley (1992) has suggested that students' learning is enhanced when they have many opportunities to elaborate on ideas through talk. In this way, students, especially ELLs, make meaning as they talk. The Think-Pair-Share strategy, specifically, increases the kinds of personal communications necessary for students to internally process, organize, and retain ideas (Pimm, 1987). In order for this strategy to be effective, however, Think-Pair-Share must be organized in order for it to be effective. Students, especially ELLs, should never be expected to effectively speak on topics until the strategy has been scaffolded for them. Some of the ways to scaffold the Think-Pair-Share strategy include the use of metacognition via teacher think alouds, ample modeling via fishbowls, and the scaffolding of each step in the process using specific techniques.

Metacognition via Think Alouds

Metacognition is defined as thinking about one's thinking. One way to make one's thinking visible to students is via a think aloud. This technique is especially helpful when modeling and beginning to incorporate Think-Pair-Share in a classroom setting. Since each of the steps in Think-Pair-Share should be scaffolded, one way to scaffold the thinking process is by unpacking one's thinking using the think aloud strategy. A good way to begin this modeling is by using an open-ended and user-friendly question. For example, if *Grandfather's Journey* by Allen Say, a book about a grandchild recalling his grandfather's immigration experience, had just been read, a question such as "What is your favorite part of the book?" may be used. Notice that this question does not have a right or wrong answer, so it allows for more language usage and modeling. Another scaffold can be the use of a reduced or simple text with an open-ended question so students can focus on the process of the Think-Pair-Share and not have to focus on the content of the material.

The teacher will want to begin the modeling process by first being quiet and thinking about the question. Many students will want to call out the first thing on their mind when they are asked to think about a question. It is important to begin with the notion that we want to become very clear, coherent, and specific about our thoughts, so modeling those characteristics will be paramount. When sharing *the* favorite part of the book, a teacher may model as shown in Figure 10.1, the Think-Pair-Share Summary.

Figure 10.1 Think-Pair-Share Summary

Nonverbal Cues	Verbal Cues
Think—Place your hand at the temple of the face, in order to demonstrate time to think about the question. As you think, try to focus on *the* most important ideas for clarity.	*There are so many parts of* Grandfather's Journey *that really resonate for me, so I really need to take some time and be silent about this, in order to select the most important part for me.*
Pair—Turn toward your partner and make eye contact.	*I'm now ready to share with you the most important part of* Grandfather's Journey *for me.*
Share—Direct the conversation toward your partner and keep eye contact.	*I think the portion of the book that resonated most for me happens throughout the text, but especially at the end, when the grandchild begins to notice, and finally confirms, that his grandfather really felt that he never belonged anywhere—neither in Japan nor in the United States. The notion that immigrants seem to lose something of themselves, both in the place of origin and in the new country, is something that I connect to because of my mother's experience as an immigrant in the United States.*

Notice that this classroom scenario breaks down each of the specific Think-Pair-Share moves for the student. First, the teacher takes some silent time in order to collect her thoughts; only then does she make direct eye contact and share only key ideas that resonate for her from *Grandfather's Journey*. Once the teacher has modeled the thinking process with this strategy, she may bring another student up to the front of the room to further model how to complete Think-Pair-Share before releasing all of the responsibility to the students with the strategy. Figure 10.2 shows the scaffolded steps for Think-Pair-Share.

Additionally, note that it is the unpacking of each step in the process, including the nonverbals that are associated with them, that will allow a student to be successful with this strategy. Putting one's finger at the temple becomes a verbal cue for the importance of really giving one time

Figure 10.2 Scaffolded Steps for Think-Pair-Share

1. **Think:** Students think independently about the question that has been posed, forming ideas of their own.

2. **Pair:** Students are grouped in pairs to discuss their thoughts. This step allows students to articulate their ideas and to consider those of others.

3. **Share:** Student pairs share their ideas with a larger group, such as the whole class.
   - Often, students are more comfortable presenting ideas to a group with the support of a partner.
   - In addition, students' ideas have become more refined through this three-step process.

Source: Adapted from Soto-Hinman and Hetzel (2009).

to be silent and think through responses, instead of just saying whatever is on one's mind. Facing one's partner and making eye contact scaffolds the appropriate nonverbal cues needed when having an academic discussion with another colleague. Finally, the first two steps in conjunction with the nonverbal cues allow one to respond fully and coherently and to make one's thoughts clear to another person. Each of these steps allows students to better comprehend, apply, and internalize information at a level that they wouldn't be able to do without such scaffolding of thought.

Think-Pair-Share Adaptation for Primary Grades

In the primary elementary school grades, Think-Pair-Share cards can be used so that students can remember when to use each of the steps. One card should have a mouth and *speaking* on it; the other card should have an ear and *listening* on it. These cards can be laminated so that they are not easily damaged. Students should hold the appropriate card when they are either listening or speaking. When a student is speaking, he or she should hold the card with the mouth on it, and when a student is listening, he or she should hold the card with an ear on it. This will be an additional visual reminder for primary students who might be precocious or get too excited about sharing their responses.

Think-Pair-Share Graphic Organizer

Another scaffold that can be used includes the graphic organizer shown in Figure 10.3 (see page 104). This becomes yet another strategy that will keep students accountable for both speaking and listening, once modeling via metacognition has been used. The graphic organizer can also be used in conjunction with metacognitive modeling, especially when students need a tangible guide for each of the steps. It is important to note that explicit modeling of how to use the graphic organizer will be needed. The following are some ideas of how to do that.

Question/Prompt Section

Notice that the first column includes an area to determine the questions or prompts that teachers would like students to think through. It is important for teachers to think through these questions or prompts carefully ahead of time so that the questions themselves require and allow for extensive talk. Such questions and prompts should occur carefully in the planning stage and can be developed with colleagues, by either grade level or department level. Questions and prompts should also ultimately connect back to the standards, content, or comprehension strategies being taught as well as the objective of the lesson itself. Questions should not be formulated randomly in the middle of teaching. Teachers may choose to compose questions collaborating during lesson planning time.

Teachers should focus on formulating questions in quadrants *C* and *D*, which ask for more open-ended responses and require higher order thinking skills on Bloom's Taxonomy. Students can also be taught to use these resources in order to formulate questions when reciprocal teaching is introduced.

Thinking Section

The second column is a section where students can write down what they are thinking about before they discuss it with their partners. Using this portion of the graphic organizer, before having students share, allows students to become clearer about their ideas. In essence, it requires students to do the thinking they'll need before they speak. Remember that even students with a lot of language, like gifted students, need time to refine their thinking. These students usually say the first thing on their mind. It is important to remember, however, that ELLs at lower levels of English language development may be able to produce more oral rather than written language. If this is the case, providing a close passage or language stem, along with a word wall for key vocabulary (if needed), may be appropriate. For example, "My idea was . . . ," or "My partner's idea was . . . ," and "Together we thought . . ." Providing students with the language allows them to focus their attention on the content. More oral language stems have been included in Appendix B.

Listening Section

The third column requires accountability for the sharing and listening process. Once students have had time to think through the question or prompt and when they share their ideas with each other, they are then required to listen carefully, in order to summarize their partners' ideas. Only after students listen carefully should they be allowed to summarize. The graphic organizer becomes a place for students to record and organize their own ideas. But it also requires careful listening and an accounting of their partners' responses. Remind students that they should not merely swap papers for this section. An example of this type of additional scaffold is "The most important part of the text is _____ because _____." Or "I completed the math problem by _____ because _____." Notice that by the addition of the *because* section of the language stem, students are required to provide more language and thinking regarding why they responded as they did.

Consensus/Commonalities Section

The final step that educators may choose to eventually incorporate with Think-Pair-Share is coming to consensus around ideas. Here, students can look for commonalities in ideas and share them. If commonalities are not present, then students should try to put their two ideas together. This section is meant to expand one's own ways of thinking and to further clarify and provide precise thinking. Since meaning is socially constructed, students' responses should influence each other via the pairing segment of Think-Pair-Share. In the end, students should have grown, evolved, and been provided with a broader perspective on an issue or question due to the sharing experience.

Fishbowl of Think-Pair-Share With Graphic Organizer

Using the Think-Pair-Share organizer in Figure 10.3, the teacher can model each of these steps in a fishbowl setting, by asking a student who is effective at Think-Pair-Share to model the process with the rest of the class, as all students look on. The benefit of this becomes the gradual release of responsibility for independent practice in pairs. This gives students yet one more model of how to complete a strategy that may be new to them. Some students may not understand how to effectively use the strategy until they see it modeled with another student, even though the teacher has been explicit with the think aloud. The more scaffolding that is done up front with students, the more successful they will be when they are expected to pair-share on their own.

Figure 10.3 Scaffolding Think-Pair-Share

Open-ended Question or Prompt	What I Thought (speaking)	What My Partner Thought (listening)	What We Will Share (consensus)
Academic language stems for speaking: "*What I thought was . . . because . . .*"			
Academic language stem for listening: "*What my partner thought was . . . because . . .*"			
Academic language stem for consensus: "*What we thought was . . . because . . .*"			

Source: Created by author, based on Lyman (1981).

Using the Power Walk for Accountable Talk

Even with the levels of Think-Pair-Share scaffolding suggested in this section, it is essential for teachers to monitor the conversations by walking around the room. This is called the Power Walk (Soto-Hinman & Hetzel, 2009), whereby the teacher holds students accountable for appropriate academic oral language development but also listens in for important ideas that can be shared with the entire group. The final step of having students share important ideas with the entire group also provides message redundancy and abundancy. Those ideas that students did not understand through their own thinking, or by listening to their partner, can finally become clearer with a third level of language practice, where they hear the explanation or thinking of another person whose response resonates for them. This layering of language and content provides the kind of oral language and academic support that ELLs need.

Teacher-Guided Reporting

Teacher-Guided Reporting is another strategy for creating language in the classroom setting. This strategy should be used when students do not have enough language to describe what they want to say on their own. It is also important to use this strategy only once all students in the class, especially ELLs, have received common information or input so that background knowledge or content knowledge does not impede the language support provided. In other words, since students will not have to focus on a cognitively demanding task that they have not yet been exposed to, they will be able to focus on the language necessary to complete an academic conversation. This strategy was introduced by Pauline Gibbons (2003) in *Scaffolding Language, Scaffolding Learning* and expanded upon in Soto-Hinman and Hetzel's (2009) *The Literacy Gaps*. With this oral academic language scaffold, the teacher will use four specific steps to get students comfortable with amplifying language as demonstrated in Figure 10.4.

Figure 10.4   Scaffolding Teacher-Guided Reporting

Strategies include

- Open-ended questions (multiple entry ways/no one-word responses)

- Clarifying questions (linguistic, more detail, complete sentences)

- Encouragement (taking language risks)

- Recasting (restating in academic terms)

Source: Adapted from Gibbons (2002).

Open-Ended Questions

The first strategy is the use of open-ended questions. Open-ended questions are questions that can be answered in multiple ways and require more than a one-word response. For example, instead of asking "Were you able to successfully complete that problem?" a teacher may instead ask, "What were the specific steps that you took to complete that problem?" The question itself requires more language to complete a full response and also allows for multiple ways to answer the question. Students at the lower level of English language development may need additional language scaffolds to complete their response, however. In this case, the use of a language stem, such as "The specific steps that I took to complete the problem were _____ and _____," can be used. This oral language stem, along with a math word wall with key vocabulary from the unit, can provide the level of support that students will need to be successful with the language exchange. Additional language stems have also been included in Appendix B.

Clarifying Questions

The second step to Teacher-Guided Reporting is the use of clarifying questions, in order to make student exchanges more complete or accurate in terms of language and content. There are several kinds of clarifying questions that can be used, depending on student need:

1. **Linguistic questions**—These questions include requiring students to use correct grammatical forms and functions. A language form is the thinking process that students will be asked to engage in, including comparison/contrast, evaluation, and application. The language function is the grammar or language set that the student will need to engage in the language form. For example, if students are comparing historical information, they may need to use the past progressive form.

2. **Detailed language**—This scaffold asks students to extend their responses beyond words such as *it*. Instead, detailed language requires students to begin to use their growing vocabulary sets. This is the place to embed new vocabulary terms or words that have been directly taught and placed on a word wall.

3. **Use of complete sentences**—This requires the teacher to ask the student to restate his or her entire response using the language stem or by having a student repeat what the teacher has already said in order to clarify the response. Students can also be taught to turn questions into complete sentences.

Each of these techniques should be incorporated carefully so that students do not feel put on the spot regarding their response. As educators, we desire that students take language risks in a classroom setting and not be so overwhelmed that they shut down. Students, especially ELLs, need sufficient practice with new language and content to be successful.

Encouragement

For students to feel comfortable in taking language risks, they must be encouraged often. In many cultures, ELLs are taught to be respectful of their elders and not to interrupt responses. For those ELLs, encouragement will be especially important because they will be more likely to speak when they feel confident about their speech. One way to bring about confidence in speech is by allowing students to practice language in pairs or smaller groups, before they are expected to share with a larger group or with the teacher. None of us want to be put on the spot, so such language practice brings about safety. If the student is sharing in a small group or with a partner, the teacher may ask the student to share with the whole group once he or she has had an opportunity to become more confident about language and content. If a student gets "stuck" when sharing with the teacher specifically, the teacher may encourage the student to keep going or provide a language stem or a partner to speak to, until the student becomes more confident. As educators, we must all remind ourselves of what it was like for us to learn a foreign or second language. We must remember that encouragement is paramount to lowering the affective filter and to overall second language success.

Recasting

Recasting is a strategy by which the teacher restates what the student has said using academic language and complete sentences. This technique should be used at the end of a language exchange between teacher and student so the ELL is able to benefit from the three other language strategies outlined previously. This oral language scaffold is another way for students to hear back, clarify, and respond to their own ideas as they are paraphrased by the teacher. It is also a time for students to feel that their ideas are being affirmed and acknowledged and that the ideas are important enough to be shared with the entire class. For the teacher, recasting requires carefully listening and summarizing the important points the student has shared.

Productive Group Work

Productive Group Work structures, such as reciprocal teaching, literature circles or Socratic seminar, are beneficial to ELLs when they are set up effectively in the classroom setting. Specifically, Gibbons (2002) suggests that there are five specific language benefits when ELLs practice academic oral language development in a classroom setting.

1. **Hearing more language**—When ELLs work with classmates in a classroom setting, they hear more language from a variety of sources. Instead of just hearing the teacher explain concepts and messages, ELLs get the message of message redundancy from their peers.

2. **Speaking more language**—In small groups, students get more opportunities to practice language in a safer setting. Instead of having language directed at them in a direct instruction approach, ELLs get to practice language with their peers.

3. **Understanding more language**—Many times, ELLs understand each other more than they understand the teacher. Teachers who know their content very well can try to explain messages several times but should also use students in the room as a language resource so that ELLs can comprehend and internalize messages.

4. **Asking more questions**—ELLs often will feel more comfortable asking each other questions rather than asking the teacher.

5. **Becoming more comfortable about speaking**—Often, ELLs feel safer speaking and taking language risks with each other.

Additionally, there are specific language characteristics that must be in place in order for group work to be in fact productive. Many times, educators are wary to implement group work in the classroom setting for fear that classroom management will go awry. Instead, the following eight characteristics of productive group work must be in place. The more that these eight scaffolds are incorporated, the fewer problems will arise as this new structure is implemented. Figure 10.5 represents the eight characteristics of productive group work, which are also described in subsequent paragraphs.

Figure 10.5 Eight Characteristics of Productive Group Work for ELL Students

1. Clear and explicit instructions are provided.	5. The task is integrated with a broader topic.
2. Talk is necessary for the task.	6. All children are involved.
3. There is a clear outcome.	7. Students have enough time.
4. The task is cognitively appropriate.	8. Students know how to work in groups.

Source: Adapted from Gibbons (2002), pp. 20–28.

1. *Clear and explicit instructions are provided.* When instructions are clear to students, everyone benefits. Teachers become less frustrated and students know exactly what is expected of them. Many ELLs come to school unsure of the rules of school and the classroom, so the more precise a teacher is regarding assignments, noise level, and timelines, the more the student will benefit. One way to do this is by modeling or providing models of what the final assignment or project should look like. This means that the teacher will want to archive students' model assignments as they are turned in. Before that, teachers may want to create sample models so that students feel comfortable about what final assignments should look like. Similarly, noise level expectations should be explicitly stated and practiced. Having a discussion with students about what noise levels are appropriate can assist with students internalizing what is expected of them. One teacher in Norwalk–La Mirada Unified School District (CA) used the volume of a song to model appropriate noise levels, as well as to pace the length of time between assignments. Finally, explicit timelines should also be given at the beginning of the assignment and then monitored, especially if the assignment will take more than a couple of days. Teachers can assist students with organizing their work, creating a schedule, and monitoring smaller components of the assignment in order to ensure success. All of these elements become helpful study tools and self-management strategies so students can become independent learners.

2. *Talk is necessary for the task.* Because we are trying to elicit more talk in the classroom, productive talk should be structured and encouraged and not merely suggested. Many times, educators place students in groups to talk and then expect them to be silent for fear that talking will get out of hand. Careful planning, structuring, and monitoring of group work will ensure that students discuss the topics that teachers would like. However, talking really should be allowed in a group setting for language objectives—what students are doing to develop their language skills in reading, writing, listening, speaking, and thinking—to be met.

3. *There is a clear outcome.* For a group task to be productive, it must be planned well and match the content objective. Students must know what their assignment is and be held responsible for it. ELLs must know how much time they will have to complete a task and what their specific portion of the task actually is. That means that the teacher will need to have organized and thought through each of these steps as well.

4. *The task is cognitively appropriate.* Not all tasks or assignments are appropriate for group work. Since group work takes ample time, the assignment must be conducive and beneficial to every student involved. That is, the task should not be so easy that it can be completed on one's own. The group work should deepen the conversation and knowledge around new skills or concepts. The group work project or activity should be planned around the English language development level of the student, as well as present somewhat of a cognitive challenge to the entire group. As per research on the zone of proximal development, the group work assignment should be difficult enough that the students in the group need each other to complete the task—at least one level above what students can complete independently.

5. *The task is integrated with a broader concept.* The group work itself should be connected to the content and language objectives being presented (see more on language objectives in Appendix B). This means an ELL's understanding and comprehension of the material should be extended and deepened by the group work discussion. In this way, group work projects and activities must be carefully thought out by the teacher so students benefit in both content and language. In other words, the group work should not be taught or presented outside of the context of the standards and objectives being introduced.

6. *All children are involved.* Group work is not productive when one person completes the entire task for the group. Many educators have had this experience with group work and therefore are not proponents of group work tasks. In order to counter unproductive

elements of group work, every person in the group must have a specific role that can be monitored and that is equally beneficial to each child. For example, one person should not be relegated to a task such as keeping time, while other students are completing more difficult roles. Instead, the teacher should carefully think through and ensure that each role is equally beneficial in content and language.

7. *Students have enough time.* When designing productive group work projects and activities, it is essential that students have enough time to complete the task well. When we give students too much time, they can get off-task. However, if we underestimate the amount of time needed, students may get frustrated. Research by August and Shanahan (2006) suggests that ELLs need more time and practice with skills and content in order to internalize them. In this way, it is essential that group work not be rushed. Teachers may consider beginning with a certain amount of time for a group activity and then adjusting that time should students need more. Using a timer is helpful to remind both the teacher and student of how much time has been allotted, as well as how much time is left for a particular activity. I typically have a timer and set it at an initial ten to twenty minutes, depending on the exercise. I then give students more time, as needed. Teachers should check with students to see if they need more time. The use of a Meeting Minder, which is a large timer that counts down time and is placed on an overhead projector or document camera for everyone in the room to view, is helpful for everyone in the room to monitor their time. Additionally, as certain productive group work activities and projects are implemented, teachers will become much better at gauging the amount of time needed to complete a task.

8. *Students know how to work in groups.* Teachers and students will only feel comfortable about working in groups when each element of productive group work has been practiced. Many educators become frustrated when students do not internalize group work structures the first time around. It is important to note that such structures must be practiced often and that the gradual release of responsibility to independent practice should also be used for success. That is, the teacher should use the *I do, we do, you do* approach with productive group work. *I do* is when the teacher models the correct use of the productive group work strategy, including appropriate structures, such as time and what the end product should look like. *We do* is when the teacher completes a component of the group work activity with the students. This could be either a mock component of the assignment or an actual part of the true assignment. Finally, *you do* is independent practice by the group. It is important that the teacher continues to monitor the group work by walking around and asking or answering questions so that students know that there is accountability for the task as it is being

completed. This is also a time to work out any kinks in the assignment or work with the group members themselves.

A Productive Group Work Model: Reciprocal Teaching

Reciprocal teaching is a manageable way to enter into productive group work because it can be used across grade levels and content areas. Additionally, since there are four roles associated with reciprocal teaching, this is an effective way to train students to work in groups and keep them accountable for the work. The four roles that are used with reciprocal teaching are as follows:

1. Summarizer—The student determines the three most important ideas from a selection.

2. Questioner—Three questions are posed from the selection.

3. Connector—The student makes a text-to-text, text-to-world, and text-to-life connection from the selection read.

4. Predictor—the student predicts what might happen next or what might be different if the main ideas within a text were used.

Figure 10.6 summarizes each of the reciprocal teaching roles, which must be taught explicitly to students. It is essential that the teacher model the correct and complete usage of each role so that students can be successful with each strategy once they are expected to complete their roles in groups or independently. Many times teachers become frustrated with group work because students are off-task or do not know how to complete the work expected of them. In this way, the gradual release of responsibility

Figure 10.6   Reciprocal Teaching as Productive Group Work

Summarizer	Connector
*Identify what you think are the **three most important events/details from the reading and explain why they are important and how they are connected.***	*Make **at least three connections** between ideas or events in the reading to **your own experience, the world around you, or other texts.***
Questioner	Predictor
*Pose **at least three questions about the reading;** these could include questions that **address confusing parts** of the reading, or thought **questions** that the reading makes you wonder about.*	*Identify **at least three text-related predictions;** these predictions should be based on new developments in the reading, and your predictions should help the group to **anticipate what will happen next.***

Source: Westerhold and Kagan (1998).

to independent practice is essential to success with reciprocal teaching. The teacher should begin the modeling of reciprocal teaching with a simple text or a selection that the class has read before. Beginning in this way allows students to focus on the strategy and not become discouraged by the difficulty of the text. Once students are familiar with the text selection, the teacher should model the analysis of the text using one strategy at a time, perhaps one strategy per day so that students are clear about the differences. For example, as the teacher reads *Stellaluna* (Cannon, 1993)—a story about a bird that becomes separated from her mother, lives with a bat community for a time and learns about adapting and acclimating to differences—she can also model reading the text from each of the reciprocal teaching role perspectives.

If students had just engaged in an instructional read aloud modeled by the teacher, she can also model a think aloud with the class in order to determine the most important portions of *Stellaluna*. The teacher may begin this process by having students work in pairs to Think-Pair-Share with a partner about the most important ideas. Those ideas can then be clustered on a web and then the class can prioritize what the most important ideas actually were. Some of those important ideas may include the specific differences between bats and birds or the importance of being accepting of those differences. Once the class has collaboratively sifted through and come to consensus regarding the most important ideas, they can be added to the summarizer portion of the graphic organizer.

Similarly, the teacher can model asking higher order questions for the questioner role. With *Stellaluna*, the teacher can model how to structure effective questions.

- What was the author's intent with the text?
- What can we learn from Stellaluna's experience with the bats?
- How does this story apply to your own life?

With the predictor role, students can consider what might have happened if Stellaluna had never been separated from her mom. Additional predictions might include what the birds might have done had they never met Stellaluna and what Stellaluna's mother felt like when she was reunited with her child. Using a think aloud scaffold, the teacher can model formulating effective predictions that advance comprehension and understanding of the text. This strategy can assist with not having predictions that are random and unfocused.

With the connector role, students can connect *Stellaluna* (Cannon, 1993) to another text they have read regarding being accepting of differences. For example, *Stellaluna* can be connected to a text on Dr. Martin Luther King. Students can also connect how they personally might or might not have been accepted by others. Finally, students can connect to a situation in the world where someone was not accepted due to their differences, such as during segregation.

Only after the reciprocal teaching strategy has been thoroughly and effectively scaffolded with an entire class should students be expected to accurately and effectively complete each role on their own in groups. Once this modeling has been done, teachers can count students off one through four and assign each student one of the roles. Each group of four will become a home group, where students will later share their specific roles. All of the same number groups will become the expert group, where students can congregate together to complete their role and come to consensus regarding their responses. The expert step, where students are grouped by like roles, provides an additional language and content scaffold so students can effectively share their specific roles with their home group.

Once students have completed and come to consensus about their specific roles within their expert group, they are now ready to share with their home group. It is important to note that this process places every student, including ELLs, in a significant mastery role. Additionally, ELLs have been given the opportunity to practice oral language twice—by contributing to the expert group and by sharing with their home group. The accountability component of having each person with a specific role requires each student to contribute to the rest of the group, because those students are needed for everyone to be successful with the material. The teacher can then have select representatives share each of the four roles with the whole class. This not only allows students to hear the material one more time but also allows them to hear the same message several times and in several different ways.

It is also important to note that the teacher should be walking around the room listening in on conversations, keeping students accountable to appropriate levels of talk, and selecting the students who will share with the entire group. Only when this level of modeling of productive group work is provided where students move from whole group into independent practice, will students truly experience effective and productive group work. Although the process may appear intensive at the outset, the training is worthwhile, as students will become skilled at in-depth conversations, which will be valuable with both language acquisition and comprehension of content.

Reciprocal Teaching Across the Content Areas

Reciprocal teaching also lends itself to expository or informational texts across the content areas. The following lesson was developed for the Santa Clara County Office of Education Professional Development Consortium for Teachers of English Learners. The lesson is a ninth-grade biology lesson on DNA. The goal of the lesson is to help ELLs transfer reciprocal teaching to other content areas, as well as to internalize and comprehend difficult concepts in biology. It is important to note that before students engaged in reciprocal teaching, a brief lecture on DNA, using visuals, was provided by the teacher. The following is a brief lesson plan of the key components of the lesson.

- **Content objective for this lesson:** This lesson is designed to help students recall and comprehend key information regarding DNA in expository text.
- **Identify academic language outcome:** This lesson will integrate listening, speaking, reading, and writing modes to help students use academic English in science.
- **Identify English learner challenges:** English learners, especially at the intermediate or middle levels and beyond, struggle with expository text. They struggle with using academic English in the content areas to describe key concepts.
- **State language objective:** The target audience for this lesson is early advanced/advanced-level ELD students (Levels 4 and 5).

The specifics of using the reciprocal teaching strategy for this lesson are explained in Figure 10.7.

Figure 10.7 Reciprocal Teaching for Ninth Grade Biology

Summarizer	Connector
In your own words, summarize three key ideas about DNA replication.	Make a text-to-text, text-to-world, or text-to-life connection to DNA replication. (For example, students might want to make a text-to-world connection between DNA replication and cloning.)
Questioner	**Predictor**
Write down three questions that you still have about DNA replication.	Write down three predictions that you have about what would happen if proofreading were not done during replication.

Source: Adapted from Soto-Hinman and Hetzel (2009).

For this lesson, students worked in groups of four using the reciprocal teaching roles—summarizer, connector, questioner, and predictor. Each student completed the following, according to each role:

- **Summarizer**—In your own words, summarize three key ideas about DNA replication.
- **Connector**—Make a text-to-text, text-to-world, or text-to-life connection to DNA replication. (Hint: You might want to make a text-to-world connection between DNA replication and cloning.)
- **Questioner**—Write down three questions that you still have about DNA replication.
- **Predictor**—Write down three predictions you have about what would happen if proofreading were not done during replication.

Once students had completed their reciprocal teaching roles using the template distributed, they also participated in group conversations discussing the material. Students used their reciprocal teaching role cards (see Appendix B, pages 130–133) to engage in a conversation about their assigned role so that they also practiced specific language for scientific discourse. For example, the summarizer began his portion of the conversation by saying, "The three most important things I learned about DNA replication were . . ." Using reciprocal teaching across the content areas ensures that rigorous academic content and language is internalized and comprehended.

The Tuning Protocol: Reflection and Accountability for Strategy Usage

Once teachers have begun implementing one or all of the three academic language development strategies—Think-Pair-Share, Reciprocal Teaching, and Teacher-Guided Reporting—they can begin reflecting on how well the strategies have been received by ELLs by analyzing student work samples using the tuning protocol. It is the power of instructional conversations, with a focus on what the student work is telling educators, which allows for reflective teaching and promotes collaboration. According to Blythe, Allen, and Powell (1999),

> The tuning protocol was originally developed as a means for the five high schools in the Coalition of Essential School's Exhibitions Project to receive feedback and fine-tune their developing student assessment systems, including exhibitions, portfolios and design projects. . . . Since its trial run in 1992, the tuning protocol has been widely used and adapted for professional development purposes in and among schools across the country. (p. 1)

Specifically, the power is in the fact that educators get to determine the focus question regarding the analysis of the student work. That is, the educator sets the lens for how the student work should be analyzed, but the student work itself also tells the story of what needs to be done next in terms of instruction. The reflective conversations had by educators around the student work samples being analyzed allow everyone in the room to benefit regarding how slight alterations in the strategy usage can create the most benefit for ELLs. Additionally, the best practices can be shared by other educators who have used the strategy in a more effective way. Using the same cycle to analyze student work over time allows educators to sustain a focus on strategy usage and implementation so that they are well supported as they try new instructional practices. There are five main steps to the tuning protocol, which are explained in Figure 10.8. Please also note that the tuning protocol has been included in Appendix B (page 137), and at http://www.corwin.com/ellshadowing, for use in a professional development or collaboration session.

Figure 10.8 The Tuning Protocol

The tuning protocol is a process for looking at a piece of curriculum and receiving feedback to incorporate into future planning.

Presentation: (5 minutes)

To begin, the presenter explains his or her work while other participants are silent.

The presenter should speak to

1. Assignment or prompt that generated the student work
2. Student learning goals for the work
3. Samples of the work
4. Evaluation format (scores, rubric, test)
5. Differentiation for different ELLs and skills levels

And then . . .

6. Ask a focusing question for feedback (Example: How can I differentiate the project? What are some interim activities? How can I teach writing skills?)

Examination of Curriculum: (5 minutes)

Silent Examination of Paperwork Provided

Participants look at presented curriculum and take notes on where it seems to be in tune with goals and where there might be problems. Make note of warm (positive) and cool (constructive next steps around focus question only) feedback and probing questions.

Clarifying Questions: (5 minutes)

Group members can ask clarifying questions to the presenter that have brief, factual answers. (Example: How many days is the project?)

Warm and Cool Feedback: (15 minutes)

Each participant shares feedback with the presenter, who is silent and taking notes. Participants identify where the work seems to meet with goals and then continue with possible disconnects and problems. They provide suggestions. Make sure to address the focus question.

Reflection: (5 minutes)

Presenter speaks to those comments and questions that he or she chooses while participants are silent. This is not a good time to defend oneself but a time to explore interesting ideas that came out of the feedback session.

Implementation of the Tuning Protocol With Schools

I have used the tuning protocol with teachers, alongside the academic language development strategies outline, in both the Norwalk–La Mirada Unified School District in Norwalk, California, and the Lucia Mar Unified

School District in Arroyo Grande, California. From January through June 2011, I worked with teacher-leaders from various grade levels and content areas at Los Alisos Middle School and John Glenn High School in Norwalk–La Mirada Unified School District, as well as at Dorothea Lange Elementary School in Lucia Mar Unified School District. All three schools used Think-Pair-Share in their classrooms over the six-month period and analyzed student work samples from a variety of grade levels and departments, using the following cycle:

January 2011: Introduction to Think-Pair-Share/Grade Level or Content Area Planning for Think-Pair-Share

February 2011: Analyzing ELL Work Samples From Think-Pair-Share/ Next Steps With Think-Pair-Share

March 2011: Creating Open-ended Questions/Analyzing Student Work Samples From Think-Pair-Share

April 2011: Analyzing Student Work Samples From Think-Pair-Share/Classroom Observations of Think-Pair-Share

May 2011: Next Steps on Creating Consensus for Think-Pair-Share/ Analyzing Student Work Samples From Think-Pair-Share/Classroom Observations of Think-Pair-Share

June 2011: Analyzing Student Work Samples From Think-Pair-Share/Classroom Observations of Think-Pair-Share/Next Steps for Next School Year

Notice that the cycle of inquiry each time included the analysis of student work samples from Think-Pair-Share. As teachers became comfortable with using the strategy itself, they also worked on becoming reflective about their practice using the tuning protocol. Throughout the six months, teachers became better at analyzing student work from linguistic and not merely content standpoints. Since the student work analyzed was mostly ELL samples, it was important to determine the students' academic language needs and not merely their content development. The ongoing analysis of student work in teacher teams provided support, accountability for strategy usage, and constant reflection over time. Since the National Staff Development Council (August & Shanahan, 2009) tells us that teachers need close to fifty hours of professional development to improve their skills and their students' learning, the tuning protocol, alongside of implementation of Think-Pair-Share over time, allowed teachers to become really good at using one academic oral language development strategy before moving on to another strategy (which was the plan for fall 2011). Again, it is not about how many strategies are being implemented but ensuring that those that are being used are implemented well. We do not need fifty different strategies in schools but a few strategies that are used well and directly support and benefit ELLs in content and language.

CONCLUSION

The three strategies addressed, Think-Pair-Share, Teacher-Guided Reporting, and Reciprocal Teaching, are research based, strategy entry points that can elicit more academic language development for ELLs in the classroom setting. These strategies also ensure that the ELL shadowing experience is leveraged into immediate next steps to systemically change practice and achievement for ELLs. These strategies are not the only ones that can be implemented to effect change, but they are the ones that have been used by the author with several schools and districts, in order to begin to change academic oral language development practices for ELLs. Only by implementing such strategies and being reflective about our teaching practices can we begin to find the language in the curriculum again, elicit the voices of ELLs in our classrooms, and begin to systemically change instruction and achievement for this group of students. As you implement each strategy, remember the difference that these strategies would have made for the ELL that you shadowed, as well as the difference that you *will* make for all of the ELLs in your classroom. Remember your Josue.

REFERENCES

August, D., & Shanahan, T. (2006). *Developing literacy in second language learners: Report of the national literacy panel on language minority children and youth.* Mahwah, NJ: Erlbaum.

Bloom, B. S. (Ed.), Englehart, M. D., Furst, E. J., Hill, W. H., & Krathwohl, D. R. (1956). *Taxonomy of educational objectives: Handbook I. Cognitive domain.* New York, NY: David McKay.

Blythe, T., Allen, D., & Powell, B. (1999). *Looking together at student work.* New York, NY: Teachers College Press.

Cannon, J. (1993). *Stellaluna.* New York, NY: Harcourt.

Education Oasis. (2006). "Think-Pair-Share" (graphic organizer). Retrieved January 24, 2012, from http://www.educationoasis.com/curriculum/GO/GO_pdf/think_pair_share.pdf

Gibbons, P. (2002). *Scaffolding language, scaffolding learning: Teaching second language learners in the mainstream classroom.* Portsmouth, NH: Heinemann.

Lyman, F. (1981). The responsive classroom discussion: The inclusion of all students. *Mainstreaming Digest.* University of Maryland, College Park, MD.

Pimm, D. (1987). *Speaking mathematically: Communication in mathematics classrooms.* London, England: Routledge.

Pressley, M. (1992). Beyond direct explanation: Transactional instruction of reading comprehension strategies. *Elementary School Journal, 92,* 513–555.

Say, A. (1993). *Grandfather's journey.* New York, NY: Houghton Mifflin.

Soto-Hinman, I. (Ed.). (2008). *Reciprocal teaching with biology lesson.* Professional Development Consortium for Teachers of English Learners. Santa Clara, CA: Santa Clara County Office of Education.

Soto-Hinman, I., & Hetzel, J. (2009). *The literacy gaps: Building bridges for English language learners and Standard English learners.* Thousand Oaks, CA: Corwin.

Wiederhold, C. W., & Kagan, S. (1998). *Cooperative learning and higher level thinking: The Q matrix.* San Clemente, CA: Kagan Cooperative.

Appendix A

ELL Shadowing Resources

ELL SHADOWING PROTOCOL FORM

Student: _____ School: _____ ELD Level: _____

Gender: _____ Grade Level: _____ Years in U.S. Schools: _____ Years in District: _____

Time	Specific Student Activity/Location of Student Five-Minute Intervals	Academic Speaking (check one)	Academic Listening One Way or Two Way (check one)	Student Is Not Listening (check one)	Comments
		☐ Student to student—*1* ☐ Student to teacher—*2* ☐ Student to small group—*3* ☐ Student to whole class—*4* ☐ Teacher to student—*5* ☐ Teacher to small group—*6* ☐ Teacher to whole class—*7*	**One way or two way** ☐ Student listening mostly to student—*1* ☐ Student listening mostly to teacher—*2* ☐ Student listening mostly to small group—*3* ☐ Student listening mostly to whole class—*4*	☐ Reading or writing silently—*1* ☐ Student is off-task—*2*	
		☐ Student to student—*1* ☐ Student to teacher—*2* ☐ Student to small group—*3*	**One way or two way** ☐ Student listening mostly to student—*1* ☐ Student listening mostly to teacher—*2*	☐ Reading or writing silently—*1* ☐ Student is off-task—*2*	

(Continued)

(Continued)

Time	Specific Student Activity/Location of Student Five-Minute Intervals	Academic Speaking (check one)	Academic Listening One Way or Two Way (check one)	Student Is Not Listening (check one)	Comments
		☐ Student to whole class—*4* ☐ Teacher to student—*5* ☐ Teacher to small group—*6* ☐ Teacher to whole class—*7*	☐ Student listening mostly to small group—*3* ☐ Student listening mostly to whole class—*4*		
		☐ Student to student—*1* ☐ Student to teacher—*2* ☐ Student to small group—*3* ☐ Student to whole class—*4* ☐ Teacher to student—*5* ☐ Teacher to small group—*6* ☐ Teacher to whole class—*7*	**One way or two way** ☐ Student listening mostly to student—*1* ☐ Student listening mostly to teacher—*2* ☐ Student listening mostly to small group—*3* ☐ Student listening mostly to whole class—*4*	☐ Reading or writing silently—*1* ☐ Student is off-task—*2*	
		☐ Student to student—*1* ☐ Student to teacher—*2* ☐ Student to small group—*3* ☐ Student to whole class—*4* ☐ Teacher to student—*5* ☐ Teacher to small group—*6* ☐ Teacher to whole class—*7*	**One way or two way** ☐ Student listening mostly to student—*1* ☐ Student listening mostly to teacher—*2* ☐ Student listening mostly to small group—*3* ☐ Student listening mostly to whole class—*4*	☐ Reading or writing silently—*1* ☐ Student is off-task—*2*	

NORWALK–LA MIRADA UNIFIED SCHOOL DISTRICT

PDA 3 & 4

ELL Sample Shadowing Agenda: Half-Day Schedule

8:00—Welcome and Agenda Review

8:15—Oral / Academic Language Development Overview

10:00—Break

10:30—Listening Overview

- Shadowing Introduction / Practice With the Protocol
- Day 2 Agenda Overview / Logistics / Student Profiles

12:00—Closing

Please don't forget to wear your <u>district ID</u> to the observation school on <u>Day 2.</u>

SANTA BARBARA COUNTY OFFICE OF EDUCATION

ELL Sample Shadowing Agenda

Day 1—Preparing for ELL shadowing

8:00—Coffee

8:30—Speaking Session

10:30—Morning Break

10:45—Listening Introduction

11:45–12:30—Lunch

12:30—Listening Continued and Practice With the Protocol

2:30—Day 2 Agenda Overview

Day 2—Meet at school sites at 8:00 a.m. (coffee at sites)

8:30—Be in classrooms by this time

8:30–10:30—Shadow ELLs in Classrooms

11:00—Back to Auditorium at Santa Barbara County Office of Education

11:00–11:30—Reflection Time

11:30–12:15—Lunch

12:15—Group Debriefing

1:15–2:30—Next Steps
- Connections to master plans and Title III plans
- Implications for professional development

ELL SHADOWING NEXT STEPS

Needs Assessment

On a scale of 1 through 5, with 1 being lowest and 5 being highest, which of the following areas do you consider to be the greatest need in your classroom?

1. Think-Pair-Share

| 1 | 2 | 3 | 4 | 5 |

Comments: _____

_____

_____

2. Teacher-Guided Reporting

Use of open-ended questions (requiring more than one-word responses)

| 1 | 2 | 3 | 4 | 5 |

Asking for linguistic clarification (grammar, specific language, etc.)

| 1 | 2 | 3 | 4 | 5 |

Encouragement

| 1 | 2 | 3 | 4 | 5 |

Recasting (restating student responses in academic language)

| 1 | 2 | 3 | 4 | 5 |

Comments: _____

_____

_____

Productive Group Work (e.g., Reciprocal Teaching, Socratic Seminar, Literature Circles)

| 1 | 2 | 3 | 4 | 5 |

Comments: _____

_____

_____

ELL SHADOWING EXPERIENCE

Reflection

1. Write a short reflection on your observation of the student's learning experience.

2. Share your written experience with a partner. Identify common elements.

3. As a group of three or more, identify common elements. Select someone at your table to share common elements with the entire group.

4. Review *Looking at Classroom Talk* in Gibbons (2002), pp. 17–18.

   a. Think about your student.

   b. Think about _____ (name of student).

   c. Did you observe your student in any group work?

5. If the eight characteristics were in place within each classroom, would the observation experience have been the same?

ELL STUDENT PROFILE FOR SHADOWING

- Picture of ELL for visual identification
- First name:
- Date of birth:
- Date of entry into United States:
- Date of entry into district:

Classes or Periods to Be Shadowed

Period/Class	Course Title	Teacher	Room #

Test Results (last three years, if possible)

CELDT Overall	Listening and Speaking	Reading	Writing

CST for ELA & Math	Grades	GPA	CAHSEE (HS only)

Norwalk–La Mirada Unified School District

PDA 3 & 4

ELL Sample Shadowing Agenda: Full-Day Schedule

8:00—Registration and Continental Breakfast

8:30—Welcome and Agenda Review

8:40—Oral Language and Development Review

10:00—Break

10:30—Listening Overview

12:00—Lunch

12:45—Shadowing Introduction / Practice With the Protocol

2:30—Day 2 Agenda Overview / Logistics / Student Profiles

3:00—Closing

Please don't forget to wear your <u>district ID</u> to the observation school on <u>Day 2.</u>

Appendix B

Academic Language Development Resources

THINK-PAIR-SHARE

Open-ended Question or Prompt	What I Thought (speaking)	What My Partner Thought (listening)	What We Will Share (consensus)

Academic language stems for speaking: "*What I thought was . . . because . . .*"

Academic language stem for listening: "*What my partner thought was . . . because . . .*"

Academic language stem for consensus: "*What we thought was . . . because . . .*"

My Name: _____ Partner's Name: _____ Date: _____

Source: Created by author, based on Lyman, F. (1981). "The responsive classroom discussion: The inclusion of all students. *Mainstreaming Digest.* University of Maryland, College Park, MD.

RECIPROCAL TEACHING ORGANIZER

Directions: You will assume the responsibility for helping your group to use one of four reading strategies to discuss the assigned reading: summarizing, questioning, predicting, and connecting. As you read, take notes based on your assigned strategy and be prepared to lead a discussion for your role in your group.

Summarizing	Questioning	Predicting	Connecting
*Beyond retelling what happens in the reading, identify what you think are the **three most important events/ details** from the reading and explain **why they are important and how they are connected.***	*Pose **at least three questions about the reading;** these could include questions that **address confusing parts** of the reading, or **thought questions** that the reading makes you wonder about.*	*Identify **at least three text-related predictions;** these predictions should be based on new developments in the reading, and your predictions should help the group to **anticipate what will happen next.***	*Make **at least three connections** between ideas or events in the reading to **your own experience, the world around you,** or **other texts.** Be prepared to explain these connections to your group.*

(front)

SUMMARIZER

In your own words, tell the group what the text said. Explain the reading in two or three sentences. Think like the author and try to figure out what he or she wanted to tell you. The others in the group will help you if you get stuck or if they think you forgot something.

PREDICTOR

You will tell the group what you think you will read about next. What is the writer going to say now? What will the rest of the selection be about? Tell the group what evidence in the reading leads you to believe this. The others in the group will agree or disagree with your prediction and give their own evidence.

(back)

SUMMARIZER

"Here's my summary of the most important information . . ."

Ask group members for additional input.

PREDICTOR

"My prediction is . . ."

"My evidence is . . ."

Ask group members if they agree or disagree and to give their evidence.

QUESTIONER

You will pose three questions about the reading to the group. These could include questions that address confusing parts of the reading or thought questions that the reading makes you wonder about.

CONNECTOR

Make at least three connections between ideas or events in the reading to your own experience, to the world, or to other texts. Be prepared to explain these connections to your group.

(back)

QUESTIONER

"My question regarding what I was confused about . . ."

"My question regarding what I wondered about . . ."

Ask anyone else if they have questions.

CONNECTOR

"My text-to-text connection was . . ."

"My text-to-life connection was . . ."

"My text-to-world connection was . . ."

Clearly explain what part of the text you are making a connection to.

TEACHER-GUIDED REPORTING ORGANIZER

Objective: _____

Content Scenario: _____

_____

Language Scenario: _____

_____

Open-Ended Question	**Clarifying Questions**
(multiple entry points/no one-word responses)	*(linguistic, more detail, complete sentences)*
Encouragement	**Recasting**
(taking language risks)	*(restating in academic language)*

Source: Adapted from Gibbons, P. (2002). *Scaffolding language, scaffolding learning: Teaching second language learners in the mainstream classroom*. Portsmouth, NH: Heinemann.

ACADEMIC LANGUAGE DEVELOPMENT LESSON PLAN

Standard(s): _____

ELD Standard(s): _____

_____

Objective: _____

_____

Grade: _____   **Text/textbook:** _____

INTO
THROUGH
BEYOND

(Continued)

(Continued)

EXPECTATIONS/BELIEFS (How will students know you have high expectations?)	LINGUISTIC COMPONENT (Contrastive analysis, standard English exposure)
SDAIE/ELD[a] TECHNIQUES (Visuals, manipulatives, graphic organizers, media)	**CULTURALLY RESPONSIVE/RELEVANT TECHNIQUES** (Diverse texts, productive group work)

a. Specially Designed Academic Instruction in English/English Language Development.

THE TUNING PROTOCOL

The tuning protocol is a process for looking at a piece of curriculum and receiving feedback to incorporate into planning.

Presentation: (5 minutes)

To begin, the presenter explains his or her work while other participants are silent.
The presenter should speak to the following:

1. Assignment or prompt that generated the student work;

2. Student learning goals for the work;

3. Samples of the work;

4. Evaluation format (scores, rubric, test);

5. Differentiation for different ELLs and skills levels.

And then . . .

6. Ask a focusing question for feedback. (Example: How can I differentiate the project? What are some interim activities? How can I teach writing skills?)

Examination of Curriculum: (5 minutes)

Silent Examination of Paperwork Provided
   Participants look at presented curriculum and take notes on where it seems to be in tune with goals and where there might be problems. Make note of warm (positive) and cool (constructive next steps around focus questions only) feedback and probing questions.

Clarifying Questions: (5 minutes)

Group members can ask clarifying questions to the presenter that have brief, factual answers. (Example: How many days is the project?)

Warm and Cool Feedback: (15 minutes)

Each participant shares feedback with the presenter, who is silent and taking notes. Participants identify where the work seems to meet with goals and then continue with possible disconnects and problems. They provide suggestions. Make sure to address the focus question.

Reflection: (5 minutes)

Presenter speaks to those comments and questions that he or she chooses to while participants are silent. This is not a good time to defend oneself but, rather, a time to explore interesting ideas that came out of the feedback session.

THE TUNING PROTOCOL

Notes for the Presenter

Warm Feedback +	Cool Feedback −

Questions:

Index

CORWIN

A SAGE Company

The Corwin logo—a raven striding across an open book—represents the union of courage and learning. Corwin is committed to improving education for all learners by publishing books and other professional development resources for those serving the field of PreK–12 education. By providing practical, hands-on materials, Corwin continues to carry out the promise of its motto: **"Helping Educators Do Their Work Better."**